Beyond Christian
Education

Beyond Christian Education

The Future of Nurturing Disciples in the Local Church

R. BEN MARSHALL

BEYOND CHRISTIAN EDUCATION
THE FUTURE OF NURTURING DISCIPLES IN THE LOCAL CHURCH

Scripture quotations marked NRSV are taken from the New Revised Standard Version of the Bible, Copyright © 1989, by the Division of Christian Education of the National Council of the Churches of Christ in the United States of America. Used by permission. All rights reserved. Website

iUniverse books may be ordered through booksellers or by contacting:

iUniverse
1663 Liberty Drive
Bloomington, IN 47403
www.iuniverse.com
1-800-Authors (1-800-288-4677)

ISBN: 978-1-4917-8166-1 (sc)
ISBN: 978-1-4917-8165-4 (e)

Library of Congress Control Number: 2015917894

Print information available on the last page.

iUniverse rev. date: 11/04/2015

CONTENTS

For Karan,
who taught me what I really need to know
about Christian nurture.

PREFACE

This writing has been a long time in the process—too long, as some of my friends can attest. I kept finding better ways to say what I wanted to say and events kept taking place that changed what needed to be said. I don't consider this a finished work, but it came time to stop and let it go for what it is.

It certainly does not cover the issue completely. There is much more that needs to be said, but I believe I have put down the core of what is important to say at this point. I plan for more to follow. In fact, in recent months the ideas here have begun to take the shape of a more intentional proposal and action in guiding the local churches into a more effective ministry.

I have been in Christian education for a long time now and have seen a great deal of change. I am sure that what is here is deeply colored by the past and I make no apologies for that. Probably the place that past will show up most is in the sections on implementing the ministry. We need to bring forward the best from the past without, however, letting it get in the way of the needs of the future. I hope you will read this with your eyes set firmly on the present and the future knowing at the same time there is much on which you stand.

I have written with my eye on my academic colleagues as well as on those in the local church. There is some detail that some of my colleagues will find missing, some because I wanted to keep it less involved, but mainly because I am just not that scholarly, to come right down to it. Someday I hope to add the intricacies that I skipped

R. Ben Marshall

over. May it be meaningful as it is, in some way, to both arenas. There is a definite focus on the United Methodist Church and its efforts in Christian education. I hope that what is here might also be relevant, however, to other Christian groups since the theological foundations at least would be shared by many of us.

If I have been around a long time, where am I coming from? I have been involved professionally as an elder in the United Methodist Church in Christian education for over 50 years. I spent many of my early years in youth ministry, as many young clergy used to do. I fell in love with Christian education from the beginning and, when I served on our annual conference staff, I became a certified "Minister" of Christian education (of which few of us are left). I was on the Conference Staff in the days (the late 60's) when there was still a General Board of Education and the structures of leadership courses and lab schools were still in place. I spent a few years as a pastor in a small church, some time as associate in mid-size churches, and the last 24 years of my active ministry in large urban churches in youth and adult education. I received a doctor of ministry in Christian education in the early 80's under the tutelage of Dick Murray and Howard Grimes, two of the towers in Christian education in the Methodist Church. In my later years I took training in spiritual direction and found an enlarged and deepened view of what Christian growth and nurture involves. Today as a retired elder and Christian educator I am deeply involved in teaching adults in my local church and hoping to have some meaningful effect on what is happening in Christian nurture in the future. I have seen us, in the UMC, go from a very large and progressive effort in Christian education to a state of confusion about what it is we are really trying to do in the local church. I call it confusion, maybe it is just change, but things are different now. Things should be different because it is a different time, but not in the way they are different. At a certain level of leadership we know that things are "up in the air," but at the local church level I am not sure that we understand what the issues are anymore in our ministry of Christian nurture. This is not a new issue. Folks in the Christian education community have been discussing this for at least forty years (and in some way the discussion has gone on since

x

the beginning). There are no simple solutions, but we must keep putting the proposals out there and work at it.

What is in these pages, though it may seem so in some ways, is not about just tweaking the system that we have, but about a truly radical effort to fulfill our calling. There are no magic bullets, no new programs that will fix it all and make us successful. The radical nature is only a dogged necessity to pay attention to God and to work hard and effectively with God in what God is calling us to do to raise up servants for God's Kingdom on Earth. Those words are often used in an empty way, but I hope that you will see in what follows that there are some very practical implications to them. I have aimed at the local church because the local community of Christians, whatever form it now takes, is still the "front line" in fulfilling God's calling in our world. If we make a difference, it must start there.

This is not a how-to manual on teaching Sunday School or using small groups, etc. It does not offer you some packaged program you can plug in. It is a big picture look at the task of nurturing persons in the Faith and some of the issues that I think are critical or at least important to the task. That big picture includes a section on a foundational theology that is necessary to understand the task. I have attempted to provide you with a look at the whole of a ministry of Christian nurture in a local church to give some awareness of all the elements involved. I do hope that local church leaders who read this can step back for a moment from the nuts and bolts to look at the big picture. That is the only way that we will go where we need to go in God's behalf.

I do express my deep dependence upon my colleagues in Christian education over the decades. What is here that is really important stands on their shoulders. I am especially grateful to those who have read and made many helpful comments on previous and present manuscripts: Jack Gilbert, former editor for the United Methodist publishing house, Wynn McGregor, a colleague in creating relevant nurture experiences for the church, Susan Bryan, a colleague and friend in Christian education who has supported me over many versions, Bill McElvaney, a colleague and friend at Northaven UMC and a leader for social justice in our nation and world, Cody McMahan, a dear friend whose intelligence and spiritual depth I so appreciate, Chuck Foster, a well known professor of Christian education now retired, and Jim Baker, who tried mightily to make me get to the point of what I was saying. Thanks also to Mary Jacobs whose professional eye contributed greatly to what is here. I am grateful to my son, John, who made the manuscript move from computer copy to ebook status. Finally, to my dear wife of over 50 years, Karan, who has nurtured me in life and in the Faith, my deepest love and thanks.

Introduction

Will They Be Servants of God's Justice and Peace?

This book is ultimately about whether the children, youth and adults who come into and move out of our Christian communities are truly helped to become servants of God's justice and peace.

Think about that child or youth in your Sunday School class who will one day grow to become a leader at some level of society. What kinds of decisions will he/she make? Will those decisions build up or tear down? Will they lead a nation into unnecessary war or lead us to a deeper more lasting peace? Will they seek to better the plight of those in need or make it worse?

Think about that adult who sits in worship every Sunday, who works in a large corporation and is faced with decisions that will either hurt or harm. What will he/she do? What have they received in your congregation that will enable them to be loving servants of God's vision for their family, their community, our nation, the world?

Think about the parents as they struggle with raising children. Will they have the insight and understanding, their own deep faith, out of which to nurture their children in the home?

All of this is to say nothing of whether the people in your congregation will come to have the personal sense of peace and meaning in life that comes from a truly personal relationship with God that God wants all of us to have.

Are these not the questions that need to guide us and push us in our congregational ministries? What is it that will transform our world if not those people who are caught up and energized to fulfill God's calling toward the Kingdom that was Jesus' vision? How our people will become so transformed and caught up depends upon what happens to them in our congregations and in their homes.

I have been involved with seeking to "grow Christians" for over 50 years. I have worked in some fashion with all of the age groups, mostly with youth and adults, and have struggled to understand what would help the persons who come to us to truly find new life because of the Christian message. I have experienced the downturn in participation in the church's life and also become deeply aware of how what we do seems to not widely affect those folks who enter the world's affairs and help them to do what is right and loving. It was not until I was moved to go deeper spiritually because of my own personal need that I began to realize what it was that would truly change people's lives and found it in the simple but difficult practice of a personal relationship with God. I came to a deep conviction that when we allowed ourselves to be truly loved by God that we would be freed to truly be the loving servants of God in the world.

What I see is that there are too many sermons that tell us to do better, to be more loving, or mouth some irrelevant theological concepts, and very few that help us to know how much God loves each one of us, which is the truly Good News of the Gospel. We have been caught up in trying to "teach the Bible" without really teaching what the Bible is trying to say to us about God in our lives. We do too much entertaining, hoping that more people will come to church, and they do, but they leave without either being confronted with the call of the Gospel or the Good News of God's love that will change them. We have simply forgotten to depend upon God working through us and in our people and seek to help what God is doing to come to fruition in us.

Years ago John Westerhoff, III put forth the challenge in his book, *Will Our Children Have Faith?* [1] and we still have not meaningfully answered that challenge. (Most recently, Thomas Groome's book is titled *Will There Be Faith?*) I am stating the question in a different way, "Will they be servants of God's justice and peace," to try to say more about the necessary result of the children, and youth and adults, having faith. We are called to not simply have faith, but to transform our culture, to bring about God's reign in the life of our world, which means to seek true justice and peace for all people.

Certainly that vision of persons being God's servants is the vision of the total ministry of the Church, so what does that mean for the ministry that we have called Christian education and that I refer to as Christian nurture? The vision calls for a true reformation in what we are doing in our efforts to "grow up" Christians. We cannot continue to do it as we have done it, as good as some of us might think that it was 40 years ago—which it wasn't really. We have to answer the question of what is it that will enable us to be those servants and what does that mean for our ministry of nurture? An attempt to begin to answer that question is the burden of this book.

Why Christian "Nurture"?

One symbol of an answer is in my use of the term "nurture." I use the term "nurture" to refer to that arena of ministry in the church that we used to call Christian education, and some call faith formation, to signal a change. "Nurture" is an older term and has not been used much in church circles for decades although Westerhoff returns to its use in his 2004 book. [2] I use it for three reasons: First, I wanted a term that could include both formation and education because I think we must put those two orientations together in a new way. When, several years ago, I began to try to use the term Christian Formation, people objected to the term because it sounded too "directive" like we were putting folks into a certain form. That does not seem to be as much of a problem any more but I still want a broader term.

Second, "nurture" has that sense of "helping to grow." It is more holistic in that we are helping persons to grow in more than one way. As we see in the plant world, we don't cause the growth of the plant,

God's creative force does that. We just make it more possible for the plant to be all that it is created to be. That is the way I see our task in helping persons to become servants of God's justice and peace. God is moving them toward that calling; we are given the ministry of helping what God is doing to come to fruition.

Third, I want to signal a move to a ministry that is qualitatively different, not what we have been doing all along. This is a different day and requires a different approach. As I noted above, I am concerned to see that all that is involved in what we call spiritual formation is fully integrated with all that we have sought to do in Christian education. That has as much to do with the climate in the Christian community as in what happens in any particular intentional experience. Christian nurture takes place in all that a congregation does, or does not do. Central to my concern is that in the present climate of reformational change in Christianity we must, more radically than before, help persons to find the center of their life in God so that all of their involvement in whatever form of community that arises will have the spiritual maturity that is needed. To say that another way, the center of the Christian life must be in God so that the community/institution does not again become the idol but that which truly nurtures the relationship with God for all who come to a community.

The Demise of Christian Education

Many of my colleagues that have called themselves Christian educators in the past will agree when I say that Christian Education as we have known it is dead. That is both bad news and good news. The bad news is that it is evidence of at least a lack of attention to, if not a complete lapse of concern for, the processes of helping persons become mature Christians. The good news is that what we were doing was not working and we can be done with it. This demise brings us a challenge to do what needs to be done for today's church and world.

Since the 1960's the entire structure of leadership development and resourcing of the local church for Christian education (nurture) has been dismantled except for a few brave souls on the General Board of

Discipleship who are doing all they can under great limitations to carry on. [3] There are many factors that go into this dismantling, but the result is that there is no longer a concerted, intentional effort to resource the local churches in their efforts to nurture their people in the faith. The staff and structures dedicated to Christian education no longer exist in most of the annual conferences. [4] There are usually exceptions in the case of youth and young adults, but this seems to be more in terms of programming at the conference level and not resourcing for the local church. That means that the tie between what is provided by the general agency and the local church no longer exists. It is also true that the local church long ago developed a (postmodern?) distrust of what came from "higher up" and went its own way to get resources from the para-church organizations that provided an alternative. Such a situation is an indication of a major challenge for the future in that there is no one resource we could provide that would fit all of the local churches. At the same time, there is a crying need for effective ministry that is not being carried out due to lack of knowledge and skill in the local church.

The lack of resourcing of the local church is a daunting challenge but no more daunting, if not less so, than the other one we face: We must completely reframe and reform the content and processes of what we do to provide nurture in our local churches. A word of history is important here: The Christian education that took place in the United Methodist Church in the 20th century was an heir to the larger Religious Education movement of that century. That movement actually began in the late 1800's when leaders in the field of education began to call for the use of the new insights of psychology and sociology in the development of educational strategy. This push to use those new insights was taken up by religious leaders in Christian nurture in the churches who saw religious growth as more of a process of socialization, a gradual growing up in the faith rather than the more evangelistic conversion approach that had been followed for so long. Obviously this might be seen as a "liberal/conservative" issue, but it is actually more complicated than that.

The Christian education we followed from the early twentieth century, and actually that continues for the most part today, is one that heavily relies on modern educational processes focused on "teaching" the Faith. It focused on the learning about the Bible and what we believe, and church history and the ethical teachings of Christianity, what we often call "schooling," but it leaves out a critical aspect of the Christian life—the nurturing of the inner personal relationship with God. You may want to object to that assessment, but I simply ask you to look closely at what happens in our present Sunday school classes. I think you will find very little learning about prayer and what a relationship with God is like and how we nurture that relationship. The element we are leaving out was actually present, however unhelpful it was in practice, in the more evangelistic conversion perspective of that earlier time; i.e., we forgot the Spirit's part in the nurture of our people. The focus on "schooling" was the objection of John Westerhoff that I mentioned earlier. We have still, forty years after his call for a change, not made it. Now is the time.

Now is the time because, even though Christian education is dead, there is still the need to help persons grow in Faith and there are still Sunday schools in most churches, and youth groups and special educational opportunities. The only question is whether these opportunities are all they could be. We often don't really understand what we are about in our efforts, we tend to want to entertain more than teach in order to gain attendance, and we are still caught in the "schooling" paradigm as I have mentioned.

Some efforts of course are effective, but from my experience, there are many that are not and that is not because leaders don't try as best they can. So what needs to happen is not just about some time in the future, it is also about now, about the lives of those in our Christian communities, about the Church and ultimately about the world. Someone noted that the church is always only one generation away from extinction.

Nurture: Inherited and Emerging

The closing days, as I see it, of the "golden era" of Christian education in the UMC came in the 50's and 60's of the last century. Those were the years when I was nurtured as a youth and came into the ministry and fell in love with Christian education. I have many great memories of what I received through that ministry as it was then—as imperfect as it might have been. I served on the staff of the Conference Board of Education and received a great deal of very helpful training and insight.

Many of you who are reading this will have no memory of what those days were like and that is as it should be. We cannot go back to those days, nor should we go back if we even could. There are, however, some aspects of those days that we need to bring forward into this emerging period of change within Christianity largely having to do with the great strides made in the last century in, and the understanding of, human development. There was so much that I gained from the church in self-understanding, in how to teach, about interpersonal relationships and how to help people that is not always a part of the training of leaders for our congregations. There was an interest in truly training leaders for the task of teaching that we seem to have lost and must regain. We will discuss some of these items in more depth in Part Three. Let's look now at some of the emerging issues and then talk about the future.

As noted above, the local church is without any clear guidance to provide effective nurture. Often what is happening is driven by the concern for membership growth or some of the latest ideas of what creates vital congregations, which may be very helpful in certain ways. The surge of interest in spiritual formation that began decades ago has taken hold to some degree in our churches with a renewed interest in prayer, spiritual growth experiences and the spiritual disciplines. My assessment is that such experiences are taking place, however, along side of whatever educational opportunities there are and are not truly integrated with the overall ministry of nurture/formation. Probably it would be safe to say that the involvement of congregations in spiritual formation is uneven across the churches in the denomination.

In a broader view we are experiencing the phenomenon of "emerging Christianity" which is an experiment with different ways to carry on the life of the Church. There are house churches, neo-monastic experiments, and other forms that do not fit the traditional mold of the local denominational congregation. This movement is a part of the view of some scholars and writers that we are in the midst of a new "Great Religious Awakening" that began in the 60's and is still slowly making its way through the Christian Church—and even other religious groups. A characteristic of this awakening is the focus on practice rather than belief: to be Christian has more to do with what we do than what we believe. This means that it is possible that folks from different theological persuasions can come together in unity in ministry to the world. What a great possibility!

At the same time there has also been a reformation on the theological side of the awakening in how we conceive of God and Jesus and the Bible, and what all of that means for what we are to teach about our traditions.

Underneath all of this is the momentous change in the religious landscape with the growth of those who call themselves spiritual but not religious, a reaction to what they see to be the hypocrisy and irrelevance of the institutional church. That is on the top of a steady decline in the membership of mainline denominations that is now reaching into the more conservative and evangelical groups.

All of this has to be considered as we look to the future of Christian nurture.

The Future

The future lies in the "Sacred Rhythm," our inward movement into a deeper relationship with God and the outward movement in service to the world in the same way it was for John Wesley in his concern for both inward and outward holiness. My central concern for the future of Christian Nurture is the emphasis on the inward movement, the person's relationship with God and therefore their inner transformation that will be the source of the power and guidance to serve the world. This conviction comes from my exploration over the last 30 years into what it is that brings people to a faith in God and a loving stance in the world. It is also because of my own personal experience in my relationship with God and in coming to understand the dynamics involved in that journey of relationship. Many years ago I came to the conclusion that if I could allow God to love me enough I could handle whatever came my way. That orientation to my personal life led me to see further that it is only as we allow God to love us will we have the courage and the power to be servants of God in the world. (There will be more about the Sacred Rhythm and about this view in later sections.)

I am sure that had it not been for the eruption of the Spirit that brought us to be more aware of and concerned about the inner journey with God that I might not see this the same way today. So a part of our emerging future that is very real and that must be taken seriously is all that goes by what we call spiritual formation. I have already noted that our efforts at spiritual formation must be integrated with the best of what we have been doing in Christian education; i.e., the best of the insights of sociology and psychology and learning theory. We can then meld those insights with the newer insights of science today such as the understanding of how our brain works. That means that the teaching about the Bible, theology, the Church, etc., will be at the service of the person's inner transformation, not as an end in itself.

The integration of "knowledge and vital piety," as one of the traditionally Methodist phrases goes, will demand a major effort to put together a new "discipline," if you will, for Christian nurture that can be used to train leaders for the future. That brings us to the very real issue of how such a new discipline or ministry can be communicated to those leaders, clergy and lay, in the local Christian communities that are on the front lines of the church. The emerging/emergent church movement is creating new forms of community alongside the traditional congregational forms. No one set of resources will fit everyone so we will need to devise approaches to training that we have not used before, such as training the leaders in the foundational concepts and the ways to develop their own resources that fit their situation.

We must begin to think about the effectiveness of what we do in Nurture that will bring about the results in loving servants alive in the world. We cannot only think about what will attract people superficially, but what will attract people in ways they need to be touched and helped. My conviction is that deep effectiveness is grounded in the person's relationship with God first of all. There are certainly other factors that will affect effectiveness, but if that relationship with God is not present, then whatever else we do will not be lasting and we will not have accomplished what God calls us to do.

At the risk of repeating myself, let me give a thumbnail, summary sketch of the nature of the task of Christian nurture that we will be detailing in all that follows:

Christian nurture for the future will be focused on the person's relationship with God and how they are loving in the world. We will leave behind the idea of "schooling" in Bible and beliefs as an end in itself for a use of the exploring of the Bible and beliefs to help persons to nurture their relationship with God and to know what it means to be loving. Its processes will be built around the conviction that God is already working within the persons we nurture and within us, and our task is to help the person to allow God to transform them. There will be a focus on practices, both of the inner spiritual disciplines as well as the disciplines of servanthood. We will take seriously the best of the insights from the social sciences to fulfill our task of teaching and working with each other. There will be a new awareness of how the whole congregation nurtures in all that it does and therefore a new intentionality to design our observances of the church seasons and traditions to create a climate of nurture in all that the congregation does that is intimately related to what happens in the small nurture groups on Sunday morning and other times. There will be a new concern for the nurture that takes place in the home and ways to support that nurture. There will be a concern for nurture across the life span so that persons of whatever age and life situation can find that which nurtures their lives with God in Christ. The congregation's efforts toward justice and peace will take a key place in the nurture experiences so that there are plenty of ways for persons to learn the ways of servanthood, hands on. There will be an effort to help our people learn that we can work with those from other denominations and even religions to bring justice and peace in our communities and world. There will be an increased effort to use the modern communication technology and social media in the service of the task. Remember that all of this must help persons to have a functioning relationship with God wherever they are in their daily life so that what they do is continually guided by God's love and call to them.

I have no illusions about the difficulty of the task of reframing and renewing our ministry of nurture, but we have no choice. We have to take up this challenge and allow God to guide us.

What You Will Find

What you will find in the following sections is my effort to give some details about the shape of an effective nurture ministry in the days ahead. What you will find is not something brand new that has never been talked about before. It is instead a bringing together of ideas and directions that have emerged in recent years that give us the foundation and direction for the years ahead that have not all been put together in quite the way I am proposing—at least that is my perception right now.

In Part One there is first a foray into some theological foundations that support the shape of nurture that I am proposing. Also, as a guide to content and practice, I have outlined what I call the spiritual dynamics of nurture that try to explain what it is that we are hoping to help happen in a person's spiritual life. Part Two is a section on what Christian nurture might look like in the local church, some of the critical issues and some guidelines for effective nurture. In Part Three we look at issues of design and structure in a local church ministry of nurture.

I trust that you will feel free to roam and focus on what seems most helpful to you, but I hope that you will avail yourself of the more theological and theoretical sections to get the grounding behind what else is here. I also hope whatever repetition and overlap you find will be a help in your understanding rather than just annoying.

Let me emphasize that this book is not intended as a "program" for a successful nurture ministry. It is an exploration of the challenges and possibilities we face as we seek to pull off an effective ministry for today and tomorrow. It seeks to provide foundational ideas and directions that can be used to build a ministry.

To close this introduction, and as a follow up emphasis to what I said earlier, I want to share a quote that has become a guiding light for me and expresses the key to whether or not any of us becomes a servant of God. It is from Thomas Kelly, writing in the years prior to the beginning of WWII. (Italics mine.)

"Out in front of us is the drama of men and of nations, seething, struggling, laboring, dying. Upon this tragic drama in these days our eyes are all set in anxious watchfulness and in prayer. But within the silences of the souls of men an eternal drama is ever being enacted, in these days as well as in others. *And on the outcome of this inner drama rests, ultimately, the outer pageant of history.* It is the drama of the Hound of Heaven baying relentlessly upon the track of man. It is the drama of the lost sheep wandering in the wilderness, restless and lonely, feebly searching, while over the hills comes the wiser Shepherd. For His is a shepherd's heart, and He is restless until He holds His sheep in His arms. It is the drama of the Eternal Father drawing the prodigal home unto Himself, where there is bread enough and to spare. It is the drama of the Double Search, as Rufus Jones calls it. And always its chief actor is—the Eternal God of Love."

(p. 51, *A Testament of Devotion*, by Thomas Kelly [5])

I have become deeply convinced that unless we can allow God to love us, to surrender to that love for us and let it transform us, we will not be able to truly be loving servants of God's vision for us. I believe that Jesus was so surrendered, and those in history who have made transforming contributions to our lives such as Martin Luther King, Dorothy Day, Mother Teresa—you name them—all made that surrender to love. That is the only way any of us will have the inner courage and the spiritual strength to risk ourselves for others in God's name. It is our task then to simply help our people to allow God to catch them. May we first allow ourselves to be so caught!

PART 1

FOUNDATIONS

What is it that guides the shape and content of our efforts at Christian Nurture? What we will look at in this section are what I consider to be the key theological affirmations and perspectives that direct our efforts at nurture, an understanding of what I call the "formational dynamics" that take place with the person as they mature as Christians, and the processes central to bringing nurture about.

It is not possible to do an effective job at nurture without understanding what is going on in the relationship between God and the person that makes the difference, and which then guides what it is that we do as those given the task of nurturing. Such "foundations" are provided by an interpretation of our Christian traditions in understanding God and what God is about. The interpretation below seeks to be a relevant interpretation for today's world but with faithfulness to the past, in this case to the Wesleyan tradition within Christianity.

The theological interpretation when seen from a more inwardly spiritual perspective provides us with the view of "formational dynamics," the content for which I take full responsibility. Spiritual dynamics has to do with the inner movements within the individual that must take place if the person is to grow to spiritual maturity. Such a perspective is important because it gives us a clearer picture of what it is that we are seeking to accomplish in being God's helpers in nurturing the individual. It is hoped that we can see these dynamics in a helpful relationship to perspectives in the sociological and psychological literature. More importantly, I hope that we can see in the view of these dynamics the very real part God's Spirit plays in our Christian growth.

When we go about nurturing our people it will be through the processes that have to take place. These processes are both the practices that the person needs to perform if nurture is to take place and those helping efforts we provide for the person that support and make possible their nurture by God's Spirit. To be more specific, these processes are the practice of the spiritual disciplines and the teaching of the necessary understandings, attitudes and skills that help the person to understand his/her relationship with God, what nurtures that relationship and how to be loving in this world.

CHAPTER 1

THEOLOGICAL FOUNDATIONS

If our efforts at Christian Nurture are to be truly effective they must be grounded in our theology, or I should say in our "working" or practical theology. If God is a part of what we are about then we need to know what we believe God is doing or not doing. Teresa of Avila notes in *The Interior Castle*: "But all we are told is what we ourselves are supposed to do. What about the work the Beloved does inside us? ... Nobody explains that part." [6] One of the glaring omissions in our efforts is our lack of dependence upon and cooperation with God because we have not really made the connection between our theology and our nurture. At the worst we don't even know how to talk about what God is doing. It is not only what God is doing, but what does all that we believe about the human condition and salvation have to do with nurture? If our theology has any relevance at all then it must be considered in how we go about our nurture ministry.

Back in 1984, Norma Thompson, writing in *Religious Education*, remarked that there does not seem to be a common theoretical foundation upon which all of the theory and practices of Christian education are built. [7] Besides the concern for what is effective, a key issue that motivates my interest in exploring a "theology of nurture" is to determine whether such a common theoretical foundation is possible. I believe that one is possible if we look to our theological roots first and fit

3

the rest to that source. There are educational theories that are important to put to use, but what we are about is more than education and must be grounded in God's activity and our resultant relationship with God. All of our educational theories should be servants to the task of nurture not vice versa. Many will say that a common foundation is not possible because there is more than one approach. Certainly there are different approaches, but how can we tell whether they are relevant to our task. It seems to me that there must be a common foundation in a theology we share out of which we develop many approaches. If you have a different theology then it would yield a different set of approaches. I offer this discussion as a beginning toward the goal of a common foundation.

The following is certainly not a complete systematic theology covering all the aspects, but only those affirmations that are related to our nurture task. The affirmations are definitely Wesleyan in their source though expressed in today's terms. Please accept the following not as the only way to a theological foundation but an effort to begin the conversation toward one. I challenge you to work on your own statement in response.

The Nature of God

Unconditional Love

First, we affirm that God is unconditionally loving. That is the clear message of our belief in the crucifixion and resurrection of Jesus. It is the proclamation of Paul that nothing can separate us from the love of God. Of course, we can separate ourselves from that love by not accepting it, but God's love for us never ceases. Richard Rohr notes that, "As history has shown, if you don't get the first premise right—God's love is absolutely unconditional—the whole thing falls apart." [8] By "thing" I take him to mean life itself and how we understand and work through life.

There are those who will want to object to unconditional love and say that it is conditional upon our repenting of our sin and accepting Jesus as our savior. Our Wesleyan bent does not allow us to go there except, that said, we can reject it; God's love is not "irresistible." God loved us, even in our sin, to act to save us, we say. That is unconditional love!

What does it mean to say that we are loved, by God or a person? I have come to understand love as the activity of building up, of giving importance to persons, helping them to feel significant, accepted just as they are. It means, at least, that I respect their personhood and do not treat them as nobodies. To say that I am loved by God is to say that I am significant just as I am, I am a beloved child of God, an heir of the promise. We will see shortly the importance of this understanding of love, which I have found to be most helpful.

Some will contend that God is a judging, vengeful God and that we must be afraid of offending God and bringing God's punishment upon us. "What about God's demands for our right living?" they might say; or "God is a demanding God, and if we do not follow the way God created us to live there are consequences, right?" To recognize that there are limits to our behavior and that there are consequences for our actions does not mean that God is not unconditionally loving. No matter what we do, or how often we fail, or how willfully disobey, God will not leave us. God will continue to love us in the midst of all the circumstances of our lives, which means grace finally saves us. God's fundamental (and only) demand is simply that we surrender to God's love. We have to finally make our decision about whether God is unconditionally loving or not and begin to live out of that affirmation.

Prevenient Grace

A wonderful Wesleyan assertion is that God's love, God's grace, is "prevenient." That older word, "prevenient," means "to go before," and it refers to the idea that God is working from within us, even before we act, to bring us into relationship with God. As Paul says, "God's Spirit is witnessing to our spirit that we are children of God." This means that our relationship with God is not of our doing, but simply of our responding to what God is already doing.

God's prevenient love fits well with the understanding that God's action is always prior. It is God who sees the Israelites in Egypt and sends Moses; it is God who is acting in the life of Jesus without our

5

asking for it. As 1 John says, it is not that we love God, but that God first loved us (4:19). To say that we are already being loved by God, that we already have what we are seeking, dramatically changes the focus of the nurture task. What becomes prior is that we help persons to accept and live into what God has already given them. If God is already seeking them, then our task is to help persons to be open to how God is prompting them toward a trust in God's love. To put it more forcefully, this means that God is the one who forms persons; we don't really do it. Our task is simply to facilitate what God is already doing in the person's life.

To say that God is prevenient means that we understand God as immanent in creation and in our very existence. God is within us and in all creation, not "out there somewhere" only intervening when called. God is within all things bringing about God's intentions for all creation. But we, as human beings, are able to resist God's actions within us as well as misread what those urgings are about. The task of Christian nurture then is to help us to know how God is working and what we can do to work with God's loving actions within us.

I believe we can say that God needs us as well as we need God. We are the agents, the hands, feet, and voice of God in history. It is through our actions that history is moved toward God's intentions. We need God because we cannot live without God's life within us, and also we cannot live in peace and love without God's love for us that enables us to overcome that within us which resists God's love. It is to that issue within us we now turn.

Human Nature

People are Created Good!

God created us and called our creation "good." That is what Genesis affirms. I take that to mean that we are worthy; we are acceptable to God, just as we are. There is nothing inherently wrong with us that would keep God from accepting us. We can affirm that we are basically good, not bad or evil.

Genesis also says we were created in the image of God. That means that we are capable, in imperfect ways, of doing what God does— creating, loving, deciding, etc. It means we are free and therefore responsible for our actions and what happens to the world. It means that we have a special relationship with God in that we can transcend ourselves, stand outside ourselves and consider what we are doing. We know ahead of time that we will die, and somehow we know that in some way what we see here is not all that there is. This is often a sense of God's presence within us, nudging us. We have a spirit, like God is Spirit and therefore there is a communication link between us and God.

In our nurture of people, we are called to see them as worthy of love just as they are. It means that we respect their individual personalities and do not try to remake them. We therefore use developmentally appropriate ways to nurture them and take care to understand who they are and what they especially need. We know them as people who have unique gifts to offer to us and to the world, and we seek to help those gifts to be discovered by them and by us.

We understand that their unloving or unhelpful actions come not from their nature, but from experiences that have caused them to act that way. They need help with their problems, not condemnation. Of course, they are still responsible for their actions, but according to their age and stage of development we relate to them appropriately as people of worth whom we respect, but who need boundaries and help to overcome their problems. All unloving actions, however violent, have a reason behind them, and the reason is not that people are "bad"!

We are Good, But Imperfect

We are imperfect and always will be so, and there is nothing we can do about it. It is simply a part of our creatureliness. Being imperfect does not make us unacceptable to God and should not make us unacceptable to ourselves, but it often does. So we have to accept that we will always make mistakes of thought, judgment, or actions. Our learning can overcome mistakes of ignorance, but we just won't always function in the way we need to or think the way we need to. We must understand that imperfection is not Sin and that we can overcome Sin, but we will always be imperfect.

What our imperfection means for nurture is simply that we have to accept people for who they are and love them anyway. We cannot make imperfections a test of our acceptability, but they can be occasions for learning to accept ourselves just as we are—which is a part of accepting God's love for us. People need to be able to know that when they make mistakes they are still acceptable.

We are Finite and Afraid

Finitude and fear are issues that go deep within us. We will some day physically pass out of existence. Whatever we happen to think about any form of life beyond this physical existence, we someday will cease to physically exist. Throughout mankind's existence this has been a deep, life wrenching concern. We have tried and continue to try mightily to work out all sorts of ways that we can extend our existence or at least take care of ourselves beyond the grave. Our physical death can be a true source of anxiety for us, although for most of our life the anxiety is unconscious and shows up only in the metaphorical deaths we experience regularly. We can say we die in so many ways: we have failed, experienced a loss, been put down or dismissed by someone else. These experiences of "death" that mirror our ultimate death become the sources of a fear of being insignificant, of being a nobody; a fear that we all have whether we admit it or not. Many people will say that is not the case, but just think about it a little and ask yourself when you become anxious, what is it that you are really afraid of? It usually is something from our past that says unless we are a certain way we will not be accepted, will face disapproval, etc. We are basically afraid of not being loved, being unacceptable to those we hold to be important to us. Such a fear is not always a conscious factor and we may have received enough love in our life that we are more secure in our self-image so we don't touch it often. This fear of our insignificance has monumental relevance to the issue of nurture and it is to that fear that the Gospel speaks.

The Human Problem

Our fear of our insignificance causes us a fundamental problem, but even this problem does not make us unacceptable to God; we are still loved. We must affirm we are of ultimate value from the very beginning and nothing can take that away from us, except our inability to accept our God-given goodness that leads to our perception of our unworthiness.

The problem is a profound one that only God's love can fix. The problem, to use the traditional term, is Sin, but it is very important how we understand what that means. The idea of Sin has been used in the past as a bludgeon to make people feel bad about themselves as a means of control. We have been told that because of Sin, we are unworthy and unlovable; this understanding has led to our saying that people are basically bad. We must do away with that perspective, but we can't do away with the problem.

Out of our fear that we are insignificant, and aspiring to find the significance we need, we try to create that significance using the people and things of the world to give us that sense of importance. Notice I said, "using" the people and things of this world. We put down others, we grasp for and even take away from others, we ravage our creation, all to obtain the money or power or whatever that we think we need to feel significant in this world. Sin, then, is trying to create our own significance or, as some have said, trying to play God when only God can give us the significance we seek.

It is crucial to understand that it is the World that teaches us this illusory path to significance. The creation of our significance without concern for others is the "way of the world" that Jesus and Paul talk about so pointedly. "Do not store up treasures on earth" ..., "do not be conformed to this world" ... and other such statements are found throughout the scriptures in one form or another.

"Why are we like this?" is a question that always arises when discussing this problem. One view is that our fear comes from the tension between our sense of transcendence (a God connection) and the consciousness of our finitude (a physical reality). To say more is beyond the scope of this writing. We can say that our desire for significance is

9

actually God within calling us to be all we are created to be, for to be significant is to actually be in relationship with God. It is our fear of not being significant and the attempt to create it by ourselves that is the problem.

We have the problem and the problem is in us; even Genesis attests to it as something coming from the deepest times of human existence. Since we have the problem we have to deal with it. I believe that our unwillingness to understand the problem and to speak clearly and helpfully and lovingly about it are fundamental issues in the effectiveness of our Christian nurture. Remember, Sin's existence does not take away our goodness and our acceptance and being loved by God.

The base problem then is our fear of insignificance. Our Sin is the result of our fear and our inability to know how to handle that fear. Dealing with our basic fear for our existence is the essential issue of any religion and especially Christianity. Fear and the resulting attempt to control it ourselves is the source of much of the human-caused suffering in the world. If we are to do away with such suffering and pain, then we must help people to deal with their existential fear. We must find ways to help people to do just that in our efforts at Christian nurture.

Somehow we must be able to talk to people about Sin, about the human flaw. It is essential to self-understanding and it is freeing when people can understand what often causes them to do what they do. The Church has allowed psychology to take over the solution to this issue because we have avoided talking about it for fear of running people off—and we would if we talked about it in the old way. Psychology has talked about the "human flaw" problem with terms like co-dependency and transference, and has sought to help people without referring to God as the solution. Psychology deals with the issue of significance in terms of self-image and ego, but without any reference to a source of help beyond ourselves. Leaving God out of the equation leads to an incomplete solution. The Church must take back both this problem and its solution. When we as nurturers can lead people to a better understanding of their fear of insignificance, we help them to allow God to transform them. [9]

Salvation and Nurture

The Solution to the Problem: Salvation as Trust

Salvation, in the Christian tradition, is the solution to the human problem of Sin and therefore the key to the presence of God's justice and peace in the world. The solution is both very simple and terribly difficult. It simply requires that we accept that we are loved and therefore of ultimate significance in this world. We "simply" have to trust that because God loves us, we are of ultimate significance to God and therefore can let go of our fear. We are "simply" saved by faith, or more exactly, by trust. Our trust is in God's affirmation of our created goodness. We say that so glibly sometimes, but it is of fundamental importance to our lives and is the dynamic at the center of the Christian message; it is the "good news." Accepting and trusting this good news is the task of the ongoing journey of spiritual growth, of sanctification.

Where does Jesus enter into this discussion? The tradition asserts that our faith is in Jesus Christ as our savior. If Jesus is God's act of love for us—"for God so loved the world"—then to say we have faith in Christ is to say we trust that God loves us. This is the "functional" meaning of the traditional affirmation.

We must also affirm here that it is only God's love that can finally solve our hunger for acceptance and love and meaning. There are many things in life and most especially the love of another person that can seemingly satisfy our search for meaning. All of those things are temporary and imperfect and will at some point not be enough to satisfy our longing for significance: for communion with God, in other words. The presence of a community of love is essential for Christian nurture, but the community alone is not enough. Only God will be enough.

When we come to accept and know that we are loved unconditionally by the very source of life itself, then our fear is overcome and we are freed from "the power of Sin" (from our tendency to create our own significance) and are freed to be loving ourselves. That is the principle dynamic behind salvation. It is not salvation only for life after death but, more importantly, salvation for a meaningful life here and now and a world that is safe and peaceful. Remember the quote from Kelly,

" ...on the outcome of this inward drama rests, ultimately, the outer pageant of history."

I said the solution was simple, but it is also difficult. The difficulty lies in the depth of the problem within each of us and the action of the World upon us to keep us from the solution. That does not mean that our culture is bad or evil, but it is certainly twisted and can perpetuate evil actions. We might say that that is what is meant by the "Fall," that our culture teaches us that we are to depend upon the ways of the World and not on the love of God. We do not need to posit another force such as the Devil or Evil to explain the bad things that happen in life. We can simply point to our fear of insignificance and the resulting culture we create to try to solve that problem outside of God. We want to solve it outside of God, or perhaps to create the solution using God, because we want to be in control. If we surrender control, we think that might mean that we are not significant.

It may be helpful here to add a note about the idea of a positive self-image as the result of God's love for us. Many of us have come to think that to have a positive self-image is not helpful, that it makes us arrogant and boastful. We think we have to respond to difficult behavior with "tough love" and not with acceptance and care. It is my belief, and I find it supported by psychology, that difficult behavior is caused by the need of the person for attention, to be respected, to be somebody. [10] What the person needs then is to have someone to say they are accepted for who they are, that they are important, at the same time that we tell them their behavior is unacceptable. Persons who have a positive self-image are the ones who will want to do what is loving and what is needed because they don't have to "act out" to get another's respect; they already know they are acceptable as they are. A truly humble person is the person with the positive self-image. The one who is boasting and arrogant is the one without the positive self-image and is trying to create it. What God's unconditional love gives us is an affirmation that we are loved, accepted, just as we are—a beloved child of God.

Implications for Nurture

The task of Christian nurture, and of the whole church's ministry, is outlined by the process of salvation. The spiritual journey is toward the fulfillment of our salvation and thereby the transformation of the world. The journey is one of coming to accept God as loving, to accept that we are loved unconditionally by God, and to be willing to give up our dependence upon the world, which is the journey of salvation. This is an ongoing journey, a process, and an intentional practice, and it is the task of Christian nurture to aid in that journey.

The importance of getting clear about our theology is that it enables us to see what must be involved in Christian nurture. It is not only the content, the concepts presented in our theology, but more importantly the ways in which that theology directs our efforts toward growing in our relationship with God. We might say that it is not finally what we believe, as crucial as that is, but the quality of our relationship with God that makes the difference. In a much earlier period in the life of the Church there were two kinds of theology. One was a more scholarly approach that sorted out the details of what is meant by the various affirmations. The second was a theology that guided and supported the person's piety, their relationship with God—a "practical" theology. As I have tried to say above, what we believe about God, the nature of God as well as the actions of God, affect how we relate to God and what we need to do to be in that relationship. If we trust God's prevenience, for instance, it makes a great difference in how we pray. Whatever your particular theology, it is critical that you become clear about how that should guide you in your efforts at nurture. It is also the case that our interpretation of the theological concepts that come to us from the scripture and the church tradition may need to take into account the way in which people function in their inner dynamics if our efforts are to be effective. We will examine this inner dynamic in the next section.

Implications for Process

Our goal is for the person to be formed as a loving servant of God's justice and peace. If we believe that we are created good and in the image of God and therefore are created as loving persons, then the task of nurture is to facilitate the freeing of the person from whatever keeps them from being loving. That requires an inner formation as well as intellectual understanding.

If God is preveniently loving, working on us from within, and if God is the one who forms us and not we, then the task is to help persons to allow God to love them and thereby form them from within. God's work from within, aided by the nurture process brings the hoped for conversion. If God's work is from within, then a prayer that enables us to listen to God's promptings is essential. Therefore a fundamental way that we help persons to receive God's love is to teach them the ways of prayer that make that more possible.

God's love aided by our love is what will free persons from the fear of their insignificance and therefore the necessity of their attempts to "save" themselves by self-serving actions and hurting of others. Our love is supported by the insights, the understandings, provided in teaching/learning experiences and practice.

One of the most crucial activities in nurture is the encouraging and allowing for each individual's self-awareness of that inner prompting of God. Such an understanding is behind the effectiveness of counseling, of the Clearness Committee that Parker Palmer [11] recommends and Thomas Groome's "shared praxis" process. [12] A simple example of God's prompting is people being more able to share where they are and what they feel in nurture settings. The point to be driven home to us here is that it is God's love working directly within the person, facilitated by the person's intentional nurturing of his/her relationship with God that will accomplish what we have always sought to have happen for the persons we serve in the Church. We can help that process, in fact we are essential to the process, but we do not finally accomplish it. To say that we are essential means that we do stand in the place for God when persons cannot allow God to touch them directly, but that does not mean that God cannot accomplish God's work without us. To emphasize this point in another way, we can say that there are two ways in which God's love comes to us that form a fundamental implication for understanding God's prevenience. God's love comes both directly from God's Spirit to our spirit within us and from God through other people to us. Both are essential to our life. Other people are not always going to be able to love me when I need it, so I have to be able to hear God's love from within. I will not always be able to hear God's love from within so I must have someone to tell me I am loved and open me to God directly again. We are a necessary part in communicating God's love, but not a sufficient part; God has to finally bring it to its fullness in us.

Love on our part is the other essential element besides the person's active relationship with God in the nurture process. By love I mean any action that builds up persons, gives them a greater sense that they are beloved children of God. In a real sense, we stand in the place of God for so many people and we want what we do to be expressions of how God sees the person. Because persons are afraid they are not enough, not acceptable, then our affirmation of the person must be expressed in everything we do for the person. It happens through not only how we personally relate to the person, but also how we plan for what happens in the nurture experiences. I suppose I have to also say that being loving does not mean, of course, that persons are not called to account for their actions, etc., but how we do that with love is critically important.

Implications for Content

What we teach about the nature of God directly affects the person's future relationship with God. To know God as unconditionally loving is necessary for the person to be willing to enter the relationship freely. One of the biggest issues people have about God, for instance, is dealing with the passages in the Bible that talk of a vengeful, violent God. It is hard for them to give up on that because they read it from a literalist perspective and many have been raised on that view of God. That is not Jesus's view of God so we must teach against that image of a vengeful, judgmental, violent God. This means that we have to relook at the way we teach about the Bible if we really want people to find that relationship with God in Christ that we hope for. We will also have to examine our own understanding of God and to let Jesus teach us something about God's unconditional love if we are not already there.

It is fundamental that we teach the immanence of God, God's prevenience in our lives. People need to be helped to understand that God is already loving them and they don't have to do anything to merit that love; they only need to accept it. They need to see that the urges toward a new life, in whatever form, come from God nudging them from within. Their response then is to turn to God for the affirmation to accept that new life God has for them and to not look to the world for it.

In general then what we teach about beliefs, whether it is about God, or Jesus or the Holy Spirit or the Church, should be that which helps them to relate to God and to know how to receive the life God wants for them. We can call this "practical theology"—beliefs taught in a way that functions meaningfully in the person's life.

The above theological perspective also means that we come to talk about Sin. Yes, I said that word that we don't like to mention anymore. We have to talk about it, however, not as we used to talk about it, but in a way that is meaningful to help persons understand why we do things that are unloving and how God then regards us and how God helps us to overcome those tendencies. To teach this is the only way that we can help persons to know how much they need God's help and in what way they need God's help.

Along with God's unconditional love we must teach people that they are good, meaning that their existence is "as they should be," they are worthy of love just as they are. Even when they act unlovingly God still deems them of worth, though they will have to face the consequences of their unloving actions. Their positive self-image is of ultimate importance and is the goal of their relationship with God because a positive self-image is the same as saying that they are a beloved child of God and they accept it fully. Our loving them is an affirmation of their worth to God and to the community; we simply back up our actions with teaching.

There is certainly much more to be taught as well as exampled that we will come across in what follows.

Salvation, Theology and Nurture

The task of Christian nurture, and of the whole church's ministry, is outlined by the process of salvation. The spiritual journey is toward the fulfillment of our salvation and thereby the redemption of the World. Salvation is not simply a personal affair, but a world-changing event.

The journey is, on the one hand, one of coming to accept God as loving, to accept that we are loved unconditionally by God, and to be willing to give up our dependence upon the world, which is the journey of salvation. This is an ongoing journey, a process, and an intentional practice, and it is the task of Christian nurture to aid in that journey.

Nurture involves our seeing theology from a practical perspective as a guide for our relationship with God. What we believe has a function in our life to guide us on the journey not to simply be something we say that we accept intellectually. Without the right kind of nurture we may never make the connection with God that we so desperately need.

Nurture is essential on the other hand to our servanthood in the world as well. Without our acceptance and growth in God's love we will not have the inner power and direction to serve as God calls us. It takes being loved by God to empower us to be loving. Nurture is also essential to our knowing how to love. Unless we know what it means to be loving our efforts will not be effective.

Reflection

What do you find missing in the above?

What do you have disagreement with and how will that affect your nurture efforts?

What of the above do you affirm and how will you seek to work differently in your nurture efforts?

CHAPTER 2

FORMATIONAL DYNAMICS

Formational Dynamics is a fancy name for the process of conversion, but one which better defines my issue here. There is a dynamic, a movement that takes place in the life of persons who enter a truly functional relationship with God that provides life and moves them to servanthood. It is foundational in that we understand that dynamic to be more effective in our facilitation of the formational process that God brings about. This is not a subject that was usually a part of our discussion in relationship to Christian nurture as we practiced it as Christian education. We knew there was something that went on, or that needed to go on within the person, but what it was never was spelled out for us. That is not the case in the literature of the spiritual life that we have become more acquainted with in recent years. In the writings of the early mystics and the more modern spiritual guides, what needs to happen within us is the heart of the matter. As we seek to integrate Christian formation and Christian education, it is essential that we become well acquainted with these inner dynamics of spiritual growth, of conversion, of transformation—whichever term you choose to use.

Let's clear up some points about conversion. Conversion is often seen as almost an emotional spasm in which we react and commit to something that we don't really understand. For some it has come to signify that we were somehow bad and through conversion became good. In some views it is the result of an assent to a certain theological position. The misuse of the word is unfortunate because, rightly understood, it aptly describes the dynamic that takes place within us in the process of Christian growth. Rebirth is another word that has been tainted by misuse, but it too, seen rightly, is a valid descriptor.

The process of conversion is not completed conclusively in just one instant. Conversion, when it is true and full, takes place over the length of our lives and is probably never complete, (whatever that would mean). A sense of new life or rebirth can take place in a dramatic instance, but that does not mean that the rebirth or the conversion is complete at that point, only that it made a significant leap forward. It is no less real for being incomplete and is always, in my Methodist theology, in danger of reversal unless properly supported.

In this section we will look at the inner dynamic first, then discuss the nature of "faith" as we need to see it within this understanding, a look at the implications for nurture from each of the movements and finally look at the relationship between this inner dynamic and a few of the stage development theories.

The Inner Dynamics

I have come to describe the inner dynamic of conversion or transformation as taking place in three movements—surrendering to Love, surrendering to God as the source of our significance, and orienting our Will toward servanthood. These movements take place both separately and, at the same time, inextricably intertwined. A separate description of the three movements, however, is important because each of them has implications for the nurture process. I am leaving the discussion of implications for nurture until we have looked at all three together. [13]

Surrender to Love

In this movement we come to some new sense of acceptance and love by the Source of Life, so that fear is lessened and there is more freedom to love and live. As I said above, this is not an all-at-once event. Our trust and acceptance begins at some point and grows from there. It may be that this experience comes through someone else who loves us, as with our parents or our friends, it may come from some experience we have, it may or may not be identified with the idea of God, but in all cases it is an experience of God within us to which we have been opened. I believe that what we experience as unconditional love, or the lack of it, from the moment we are born, if not before, functions to build or hinder our trust and therefore our positive self-image. People who come to us in our churches are at all stages of having this sense of love and acceptance. In the times when we sense a new surge of trust and assurance that we are loved, theologically we can call this movement a time of "justification," meaning that we feel right, in place, with God and the world because we feel loved and accepted. Usually this kind of wonderful sense of rightness does not last for an endless period, but it seems that we are on "higher ground" than we were before. Use of the word "conversion" would be in the sense that we have been converted from some level of fearfulness to a deeper sense of being loved.

I hope that you have been able to see the fundamental nature of this movement from the above theological discussion. God's love is constantly coming to us to give us life. It is that love that both helps us to overcome our fear (which causes our unloving actions) and to love those about us. The conversion from that fear to trust is fundamental to what else happens within us.

Changing Our Source of Love

From the day we were born, along with whatever degree of our being loved unconditionally, we are also taught directly and indirectly that to be OK, to be accepted and loved, we must perform to some level of expectation that has been set by those we see to be in charge of our acceptance in life. This can happen through our parents, unwittingly, because they are also caught in the same web of expectations, and it certainly happens in the culture at large. Our culture is created out of the complex involvement of humans who are all functioning under the "power of Sin" to some degree or another. That is the "way of the world" as over against the "way of the Spirit." Our learning this need to perform to certain expectations is the "sea in which we swim" as human beings.

The conversion that takes place in this movement, then, is the move from depending upon the world for our significance to depending upon God for it. Through our being nurtured, we slowly learn to trust in God's love, thereby becoming able to depend upon God and not upon what the world says about us. We are able to do this because we come to know we are loved, but it is a distinct aspect of conversion that we need to be aware of because it calls upon us to help people become aware of our dependencies as well as our fears. It is a function of the spiritual journey to let go of those dependencies and attachments and to allow God to provide the significance we crave. It is, therefore, an intentional effort on our part to let go as well as depending upon God to bring about that letting go within us.

Let me quickly say that a Devil or Evil Force is not responsible for the "way of the world." We are responsible for it! Our collective Sin is what is functioning here and it operates out of the collective sense of fear that exists in our communities. There is no scapegoat here. The relationship with God is not one that is only comforting but also confronting; it confronts us with where our dependencies and our attachments really lie over against where God calls us to be. Remember too that when we see those individuals, communities and agencies which are seeking to live in the way of the Spirit and the difference they have made in our world, it is a witness to God's activity within the persons who make up those groups and activities. Without them we would not have many of the arenas of compassion that we do have.

Orienting Our Will to Servanthood

Here we enter an aspect of conversion that is different from the other two because it includes the intentional experience on our part of being loving. It involves an understanding of the nature of love, the skills with which to be loving, and a shaping of our intentions toward ourselves and others and creation.

The shaping of our intention begins with the content of our spirit, whether we are afraid and have to defend our significance or whether we are trusting and free to reach out in love. As we are guided in the ways of love and gain a sense of significance in being loving our intentions are shaped toward the ways of love. We may talk about this as a development of our conscience toward being loving and the development of loving habits in our living. We have all experienced being confronted with a choice of what to do and feeling that tug to be unloving, but then we feel the stronger tug to be loving and decide to act upon it.

Once we have begun to trust the love for us from God and others, it then takes understanding the nature of love for us to discern how God really wants us to live. Having some idea of what it means to be loving in different situations comes through guided experience in the home and in the Church.

We are born able to love and really wanting to love, but we are not necessarily born knowing how to love, even when we feel loved enough to be free to love. We have to teach our children, for instance, that there are certain more loving ways to get what they want than others—that people are not for hitting or misusing, etc. It is not that our children don't want to be loving, but they just need to know how to go about it, and that need extends throughout our lifetime. If we are to be loving in a particular community concern, for example, how is it that we should vote this time? How do I handle the situation in the office in a loving way? What does it mean to build systems in our society that are just?

Remember that fear can always enter here. We are usually only unloving when we are afraid that we will not have what we need. Our tendency to Sin comes in and we put others down in some way to get what we want. Therefore the conditions to truly be loving even after we have come to know how, depend upon our maturity in knowing we are loved but also through the community with which we surround ourselves.

The Nature of Faith

Before we talk about the implications of this dynamic for nurture efforts it is important to understand what we mean by "faith." We have said that our relationship with God in which we accept God's love for us is the answer to the problem of our seeking to create our own significance, and we usually use the word "faith" to talk about that relationship. We then can say that Faith in God is having a relationship with God. The word, however, is used in different ways in the Scripture, and it is so because a relationship has different aspects to it that correspond to how we as humans function inwardly.

There are three aspects or orientations of the word faith: cognitive, affective and conative. (There are various terms used for these three aspects, but they are all talking about the same phenomenon.) Just so we are clear let's define those terms: Cognition involves our intellect, our thinking and our knowledge. Affect deals with our feeling, our emotion, and, in my theoretical perspective, our self-image. Conation is the least familiar; it stems from the Latin *conatus*, meaning any natural tendency, impulse, striving, or directed effort. To better understand how we function we can think in terms of three "faculties" that we all have that correspond to these three facets of faith—the faculties of Intellect, Spirit and Will. Our Intellect has to do with cognition, our Spirit goes hand in hand with our affect, and our Will corresponds with the conative. In the Scriptures the three ways that faith has been used are related to these three faculties: faith as intellectual assent (we often use the word "belief" for this though that is not all that "belief" can mean); faith as trust; and faith as loyalty in action.

The relating of our Spirit to our self-image and to trust is very intentional and central to an understanding of the dynamic. It appears to me that our affections, our emotions, and our inner motivations arise from our self-image, which is directly related to our sense of being accepted, loved, trusting our significance. The faculties of the Intellect and the Will interact in a complex way in forming the state of the Spirit and also in expressing that Spirit. For example, what we learn cognitively about God affects how we begin to feel about God and our willingness to be in a relationship with God. Our actions in being loving or not also affect the Spirit positively or negatively. The Spirit in turn motivates our Will and our search for further understanding. This view offers a helpful way to talk about our spiritual dynamics and thereby inform our nurture efforts.

Looking at faith from this three-fold perspective is important because it helps us to see that we must be intentional about designing nurture experiences that touch all three faculties. At the same time it is critical to understand that the most basic faculty is the Spirit because this is the one that needs to be touched most deeply by a growing personal relationship with God, by experiences that communicate love and acceptance to the person affectively and not just intellectually. The central arena of inner transformation is in the Spirit, in our self-image. That means that our experiences must include these more affective aspects of unconditional love, of receptive prayer, etc., along with the experiences of information reception and practice in loving actions. They all are critical and we cannot depend upon just one or even two of them as we have too long tried to do.

Implications for Nurture

Let's look now at what needs to happen in our nurture efforts to facilitate the three movements described above. Remember that they occur in a constant interactive manner so to separate them is artificial but necessary to understand what has to be involved in nurture experiences. Risking the danger of this becoming tedious, I have noted the implications of each movement as they take place for each of the three faculties so that we can better understand how to use the faculties to talk about aspects of nurture experiences.

Movement 1
Surrendering to God's love makes the other two movements possible because in surrendering, we enter a truly functional relationship with God. I cannot emphasize enough the necessity of the person's relationship with God to ultimately fulfill this movement insofar as it is possible. Therefore this movement is prior to all others just as God's love is prior in all things.

Movement 1: Spirit

The affect, the Spirit, the self-image, is the central arena of nurture for this movement. Our self-image is affected by intellectual content, but not as powerfully as by how we are treated relationally and by our relationship with God. The result of knowing that we are loved unconditionally is a positive self-image, a sense of being accepted as I am, of being enough. A positive self-image is fundamental to our freedom to be loving.

Our coming to know God's love potentially begins the moment we are born if not before. All developmental studies point to the fundamental significance of the first 3 to 5 years of life in the development of the inner lives of individuals, how well they respond to life and what they will do with their lives. This is no less true in the spiritual realm. If the growth of one's positive self-image is the key and the same as one knowing oneself as a "beloved child of God" then this is a foundational time for the growth of such a self-image. Erik Erikson's first psychosocial developmental task which takes place in infancy the person developing fundamental trust or mistrust of their place in life. In other words, infants come to perceive whether they are important in this universe and begin to respond to life on the basis of that perception. This means that the kind of early parenting the infant receives is crucial for that child's spiritual growth. The love called for here is an unconditional love for the child, a challenging task for the parents. Of course, the task of the parent and then the caring community does not end with infancy, but continues throughout the lifetime of that person.

It is critical for us to remember that the persons who come to our congregations are in all stages of how they see themselves. They can be very distrusting or they can be positive and open and all levels in between. I cannot emphasize enough the crucial nature of this aspect of nurturing our people in their Spirit.

To treat the persons who come to us with respect and caring has always been understood as fundamental in the Christian community. That is because it is fundamental in the spiritual dynamic of a person becoming a servant of God. A person sees the Church as the extension of God. Therefore, how one is treated in the Church speaks to how God treats the person. If then we want the person to become close to God, to know God as loving and accept that love, then those who represent the Church must show unconditional love as far as is humanly possible.

Showing such love happens in many different ways. As we have mentioned, it comes through personal relationship, the way we treat each other, which includes language of course. It can also come in the ways we provide developmentally appropriate experiences, both content and method, that take into account the age and situation of the person. Love is shown as we provide an emotional climate in groups that are open, accepting, that encourage questions and accept doubts. All of this has to do with whether persons feel they are important to what happens in the Church. Love is about building up one another's significance, while at the same time calling forth responsibility from each other.

Finally, the issue is about how we help the person to personally accept love from God. At the affective level that involves the person praying in a way that engenders that acceptance which we noted as something that needs to be learned intellectually and then practiced. In the practice is where the person's Spirit becomes open to God's love and that is the ultimate of what we seek for this movement.

Movement 1: Intellect

For us to be willing to surrender to God's love, we must intellectually understand that God is an unconditionally loving God. This involves some very intentional sessions in which the person is helped to look at the scriptures and the tradition that holds that affirmation. The problem is that there are a lot of scriptures and a lot of tradition that seems to say otherwise. That means that at certain ages we have to be very selective and at others very affirming of the reality of that unconditional love. For many people their past experience both in the church and outside of it has been anything but unconditionally loving. It may take special efforts in nurture to counteract those experiences. We must seek to behave in ways that reflect God's loving nature, and we must work to explain the Biblical content which seems to contradict this message. One of the big theological blocks, for instance, for many is the idea that God caused his own son's death to accomplish salvation.

They just don't see that as loving and they have not been helped to see it any other way!

One of my greatest complaints about the present state of preaching in the Church is that we tend to emphasize what people need to do rather than how much God loves them. If people hear only what it is that God calls them to do, how will they have the inner spiritual energy received from God's love to do what God calls us to do. Who wants to come, Sunday after Sunday, to be pummeled with demands for our time and effort and never hear a word about how important they are?

Another basic element in speaking to the person's Intellect is encouraging the person to see himself or herself as worthy of being loved. A key to someone's acceptance of the tenet that God loves them is to see themselves as worthy of that love. Therefore, the task of nurture is to provide people with the concepts that support their coming to understand themselves as "God's beloved children" and other such labels from the Scriptures.

A part of the intellectual content in nurture must be teaching the concepts of receptive prayer. Too often we only teach a kind of prayer that involves petition or supplication and not ever mention a prayer of receptivity. Learning to be receptive in prayer is fundamental to the deep acceptance of God's love.

Persons need to be helped to name specific situations where they are most likely to receive and experience God's love, both through others and directly from God. Identifying these situations is another way to engage the person's Intellect.

Movement 1: Will

The movement of accepting God's love is carried most fully by the faculties of the Spirit and of the Intellect. The Will or intention is involved in simply committing one's self to pray and to putting oneself in the places where one can receive that love. We who nurture must guide the person toward a regular practice of the disciplines and the way of receptive prayer, as well as developing the habits of being where God's love is most clearly caught. Our encouragement of such practices must be given a high place alongside our encouragement toward social and ethical actions.

Movement 2

How can we call people into account within this shelter of God's love in a way that they are able to change their source of significance from the World to God? Beyond accepting God's love, the central event in a person's transformation or conversion is this change in the source of our significance. But calling people to change necessitates our confronting them with their attachments to the world. Such confrontation is fraught with the dangers of seeming excessively judgmental and making people feel badly about themselves in the midst of trying to convince them that they are loved unconditionally. The ability of persons to be open to being confronted with the need to change will depend upon the degree they have come to trust that God loves them. Each of us has to feel emotionally secure to be able to examine our dependencies.

Movement 2: Intellect

The intellectual content involved in this second movement has to do with helping persons understand what is happening when we do what we do. It is a lesson in self-understanding. Such lessons usually best take place by first talking about why people do what they do in general for only individuals can talk about why they do what they do in any particular situation. If they are asked to do so it has to be in an emotionally safe environment where others are doing so in the light of some theoretical examination of situations.

The content also needs to involve what the Scriptures mean when they talk about the way of the "World" or the difference between the "flesh and the Spirit" as in Paul's discussion in Galatians and elsewhere. Such an understanding will help to provide a background for talking about this issue in the first place. We should be able to discuss here the whole understanding of conversion and transformation in a way that is intellectually sound and without any judgmental overtones of condemnation. This is also the function of understanding the commandments and prophetic teachings as they point out the conflict between our relationship with the culture and our relationship with God. In discussing this conflict the emphasis should not be on how we should act but rather on how these teachings help us to understand our human situation. We will deal with the ethical teachings from a different perspective in Movement Three. It is helpful to understand the function of our culture and how it seeks to gain our dependence and why God is the only source of what we truly need and want—love and acceptance and peace.

The teaching that is related to the person's prayer, then, has to do with understanding how to do a self-examination in prayer to uncover our fears and our control efforts in receiving and accepting God's love. It is a part of our human problem that we tend to reject the simple surrender to God's love because we believe that we have to control it, otherwise we will not be "good enough." Therefore it is very important to be able to uncover our fears and lack of willingness to surrender to the love.

Movement 2: Spirit

Movement Two is the response to acceptance of God's love and is made possible by that acceptance. In prayer the person becomes able to examine his or her life. In doing so they see their fears of insignificance and their efforts at control and the need to surrender that fear and control to God. This happens, of course, over a lifetime and, though there can certainly be tremendous progress in the various conversion moments, it is never finished.

What is taught about this movement in prayer can be supported and guided in various kinds of retreats or group sessions to nurture the inner life. Such times of guided practice help people then to develop important habits they can use in their private prayer. Such movement is also aided by one to one spiritual guidance with an experienced spiritual guide/director. It can also happen in a mature spiritual friendship with another person. Learning to become self-aware is critical so that people can look at themselves becoming aware of how they feel in all situations in life.

Corporate worship can also play a powerful part in this movement both in the content of the guidance provided by a sermon and, just as importantly, by the movement of the ritual throughout the service. A flow of images and responses by the people can be very helpful to see where they are and to experience the love and trust that God is calling them toward.

Movement 2: Will

The orienting of the Will in Movement Two consists basically of helping our people to see the importance of regular participation in the spiritual disciplines and their gaining a clear picture of how our culture functions in light of what God is inviting us toward. For people to want to depend upon God, besides knowing they are loved, they must have clear reasons that make sense in today's world and then be called to commit themselves to such dependence and love. It is important to create a culture within the congregation that sees such inner work and a personal relationship with God as of central importance.

The individual might be helped to practice becoming aware of and letting go of certain kinds of actions that express a dependence upon the world and not on God. They might then begin to question why they are buying certain things. "Do I need it or am I buying it to feel good about myself? Am I trying to do something at the office that will engender approval of me even though it is wrong? And what about relationships; are there times I try to get people to like me because I need their approval?" These are tough issues that take some deep self-awareness and receptive prayer to work on.

Movement 3

It is one thing to want to be loving, and quite another to actually be loving in our living. Even though we feel love we may not know how to be loving in any particular situation. This Movement, then, involves some heavy work on content and some very intentional practice of the ways of loving.

Movement 3: Intellect

The content supporting this movement is again focused on the lifestyle teachings of Jesus, the commandments and the prophetic material. This time the focus, however, is on shaping our Christian living in the world going beyond understanding the conflict between the world and the spirit. Here is where we begin to talk about the giving of ourselves in the light of what God has given us. We begin to talk of servanthood and of calling or vocation.

This is an area where we have been very good about covering the material so we should have little trouble coming up with the resources. As I have noted, however, we have failed to pay attention to the centrality of the other two aspects of transformation and have expected people to pull off the command to love others without first being completely grounded in the concept of how much God loves them, which is counter productive.

There is a tendency for us humans to believe that there are always options for our actions and that we can do anything we want without consequences. A major learning in this arena of Will and intention is to understand that there are certain "laws" built into the very fabric of the universe which are expressed as the "commands of God" or the teachings of Jesus and disobedience to those commands will bring consequences that we do not want. Unfortunately, even when we learn what is loving, our fear and our desire for significance overcome our knowledge and we act unwisely and harmfully. It is therefore only as we can overcome our fear, through God's love, that we will be free to be obedient.

We must talk about what love is and how it is shared with others. What does it mean to love our enemy or the one who is different? How do we show love in the political arena or in the family? Such content should cover all the areas of living and be provided for people across all ages in ways relevant to where they are and their concerns.

It is important to talk about the relationship between our reception of God's love and our ability to be loving. It is so important to continually emphasize the necessity of God's part in what is going on with us and through us.

Movement 3: Spirit

The inner work in this movement is carried on in guiding one's reflections and prayer about the situations we face in life. Also included in the discussion are the ways in which we have tried (and sometimes failed) to be loving in daily life. The ways in which we encounter people who are in need and seek to help them can move us within; that needs to be shared and affirmed as a part of our Christian path. Such experiences confirm our commitments to being servants and also attests to the presence of God's love in all our lives.

We can help the person to strengthen their commitment to servanthood. One way to do so is by encouraging people to bring their fears and concerns about servanthood to their prayer and to let God love them and "speak" to them about those issues. Also, our prayer can help us to be more discerning about our efforts at being loving. Knowing we are loved not only frees us to be loving to others, but it also helps us to be the kind of servants that are needed in the situation and not simply be there for our own satisfaction.

In actual servanthood experiences the practice of prayer and corporate worship related to the service being done is a way to help persons touch their Spirit with God's Spirit and confirm their servanthood.

Movement 3: Will

The actual practice of servanthood is fundamental to orienting the Will to being loving. It is in such experiences that persons gain confidence in being loving and in discovering the results of such servanthood in their lives which is a powerful orienting process

It is critical that when we involve persons in servanthood experiences, we provide plenty of occasions for reflection on those experiences, individually and as a group. We help the participants focus not only on their inner experiences, but also on what happened and how well we were servants in the particular situation. That way we get down to the hard reality of what it means to be a servant in the world. So much potential nurture is lost if we do not provide such reflection time. Another powerful experience is the opportunity for persons to make a personal, public commitment to servanthood in the context of the congregation's worship. What if we affirmed our people's servanthood personally on a regular basis by recognizing what they are doing in the world as well as in the Church? Many congregations have sending rituals when groups go on mission trips. Could we not extend that to individuals who stay at home and serve? Also, how about opportunities for youth, as high school and college graduates, to recommit themselves to the Christian path as they move into the next stage in their lives?

Spiritual Dynamics and Christian Practices

The spiritual disciplines are the heart of bringing about the movements of the Spirit. They are the heart because the relationship with God is fundamental to such movements and the disciplines are specifically focused on nurturing that relationship with God. It is the case, however, that there must be guidance of the content of the disciplines if they are to contribute more effectively to the movements.

The interpretation of the inner dynamics that I have shared is a reflection of a tradition of spiritual formation that has come about over the centuries as Christians have reflected on the Gospels and dealt with the experience of God in their lives. At the same time this interpretation is not necessarily held by all Christians. For example, many Christians see the purpose of prayer as mainly petition, supplication, and thanksgiving and not as surrendered receptivity to God's love. I certainly do not believe that the movements described above cannot take place in a person of different orientations to prayer—God's grace comes in many ways. But I have come to believe that as we seek to guide persons in their spiritual growth we must come to use the perspective I am proposing if we are to be more helpful in nurturing servants of God's Kingdom.

I make that claim because, as I have sought to explain, it is only as persons truly enter and nurture a relationship with God in which they come to accept God's love and trust it more and more completely that they will become the loving servants God calls us to be. Some quotes, besides the one from Thomas Kelly that, to me, support this view:

In the Gospel of John we find Jesus saying to Peter who resists having Jesus wash his feet, "Unless I wash you, you have no share with me." (John 13:8, NRSV)

John Wesley writes:

"We must be holy of heart, and holy in life … But we must love God before we can be holy at all: this being the root of all holiness. Now we cannot love God, till we know he loves us. "We love him, because he first loved us." And we cannot know his pardoning love to us, till his Spirit witnesses it to our Spirit." [14]

From Evelyn Underhill:

"…I feel, more and more, the danger in which we stand of developing a lopsided Christianity so concentrated on service, and on this-world obligations, as to forget the need of constant willed and quiet contact with that other world, from whence the sanctions of service and the power in which to do it proceed." [15]

So we must surrender to God's love and it is a prayer of receptive surrender to that love that brings that relationship with God in its fullness. Of course, that prayer is fed by the scriptures, the sacraments, the worshipping and caring community, and it's result is expressed in the practice of doing no harm and doing all the good we can.

I take as the best expression of the spiritual disciplines those called for by John Wesley in the "General Rules" in order for us to "work out our salvation." I believe that the movements described above follow the implied movement found in the list of disciplines that have the two-fold movements of inward to the relationship with God and outward in love for the world. There is not a direct correlation, however, because what I am describing in the movements is what is happening, or hopefully happening, within persons as they grow in their relationship with God. What the disciplines describe are the outward practices that are found to bring about those movements.

There are many forms of prayer that are helpful and we have to learn what is helpful for us in particular. I find it fundamental, however, to learn some form of receptive prayer where we allow God to love us, to give us what God wants to give us. Otherwise we miss the most important part and miss the gift altogether.

In studying the scriptures it is important that people find the passages through which they can see how much God loves them and be able to not get lost in those segments that pronounce some kind of judgment, etc.

In the sacraments is it crucial that persons see them as signs of God's love for them, that they are fed spiritually at God's table as honored friends fed with the food they truly need.

In worship there should be a structure, a flow, that helps the congregation to recognize where they are spiritually and then hear and receive the good news of God's Love as well as the call to go out as servants.

Without this kind of focus and guidance through the disciplines, we will not be as effective in our task of nurture as we are called to be and the Church's mission will falter even further.

Spiritual Dynamics and Theories of Faith Development

Any discussion of spiritual growth must deal with the various stage developmental theories that exist and are being created. Some of these descriptive stage development images of human growth are out of the psychological disciplines and some out of a religious orientation. The most well known of the religiously oriented images is James Fowler's description of the stages of faith. [16] You can go as far back at least as Teresa of Avila [17] and as recent as Richard Rohr.[18] All of these are descriptive not prescriptive stage development images of spiritual growth. They describe the different stages persons seem to go through on their spiritual journey. They each have their own value with none being definitive nor absolute in their descriptions. No person is a perfect match for any of the stages at any one time.

These theoretical images are helpful for us to understand that we all are at different places on our journey for various reasons. They are therefore a potential source for self-understanding which is critical information for our journey. It is helpful unless, of course, it becomes a value-laden view of our growth and used to say that we need to be somewhere else than where we are and, therefore, we are not acceptable. It is very important to not try to put people in a box in one of the stages. It is more helpful for them to see the stages and decide where they are, if anywhere, and to know that to be somewhere else is perfectly okay!

The suggested stages cannot be related one-to-one with the movements that I have described above. Salvation is not a developmental process; it does not take place as a matter of course in our lives, but comes about through our openness to God's actions in our life. The movements involved in conversion happen over and over again and are, however, at the base of any of the moves from one developmental stage (in the psychological category) to another. If the conversion is going on, the person will be moving through the stages because spiritual maturing facilitates positive movement in the stages.

In Fowler's descriptions, which I am most familiar with, the stages have a definite relationship with the person's cognitive development. In Erik Erikson's stages of psychosocial development [19], the psychologically oriented one I have used most, the descriptions are related to social roles. Both of these stage images are pictures of a person's potential movement during his/her lifetime, but also can be understood as describing movement at any one point in time.

It is my contention, however, that the growth process in both are motivated by the affective dynamic in us—what I have called our Spirit. They both, underneath all else, have to do with self-image in moving from one stage to another. That is especially evident in Erikson's schema in the polar juxtaposition of each developmental task. Self-image as motivation is less clear in Fowler's stages, but is the only motivating force I can see. What occurs is that when one reaches a new level of positive self-image, one becomes free to move to a new stage when confronted with a changing life situation. If their self-image is more negative they will tend to retrench themselves in the more comfortable position. One can get stuck in a certain stage just as we can say one's spiritual journey can be side-tracked. That, of course, does not mean they are any less loved by God, and we will know them by their fruits.

Finally, the various stage development theories that have to do with physical, cognitive, moral, etc., development are important for those who nurture others to know about because they give us indications about what is developmentally appropriate and what we can expect from those in our care. For instance, cognitively we cannot generally expect a youth less than 12 years of age to be able to comprehend abstract ideas and metaphor as well as those older. We cannot expect young children to be able to sit still for long periods. Youth are going through various aspects of identity formation which affects the way they act in certain circumstances. We could go on, but simply know that if we understand something of the various stage development views of our people, we will be better able to provide effective experiences for them.

Review and Implications

The three movements described above as the inner dynamic of conversion are an attempt to express what happens in the spirit of persons when they are on the journey toward being God's servant, a follower of Jesus, in light of how we understand God is working with us. How that happens finally is a mystery because God is a mystery, but we are charged with the task of facilitating what God is doing so we somehow must try to understand what we are called to do. We are called first of all to help persons to enter their own, personal relationship with God and to do so in a supportive, loving community. We are then called to guide those persons in knowing how to let God love them, to become aware of their barriers to that love and their dependence on the world rather than God. We go on to help them to orient their lives in dependence on God and not on the world and how to be loving in the world around them.

All of that happens as we help them through providing experiences and teachings that communicate through all three of their faculties of Intellect, Spirit and Will. As we help we are also aware of how the stage of life development they are experiencing needs to shape the experiences and teachings we offer. In this mix of faculties and stage development through which we seek to facilitate the movements, we work out how the task of teaching (education) interacts and works with the spiritual practices that are so crucial to the whole of Christian nurture.

CHAPTER 3

NURTURE AND THE GUIDING AND TEACHING PROCESSES

We have discussed the inner dynamics of formation, that is, what happens within the individual in the process of conversion. Next we will discuss processes of nurture that facilitate God's work in the person's life toward conversion. The process has two components: first, the guidance of those experiences through which the individual "self-nurtures" a relationship with God intentionally; and second, the process of teaching that provides the preparation and support for the inner change and the task of servanthood. Regarding the first component, I refer to "intentional" nurturing because our relationship with God is engendered by God through many experiences without our also intentionally facilitating that change. This relationship between education and spiritual guidance is what I have been promoting as the essential nature of the nurture process for the future.

Guiding the Inner Journey

The first component we mentioned is the person's actual, intentional practice of the spiritual disciplines both privately and corporately. We have not considered this a necessary element in the nurture process in the past in the same way we have the learning of the content of the

Christian tradition. We have spoken of its importance, but not seen it as something we make a major effort to bring about. It is actually the most important part of the Christian journey of growth since it is in the person's private and corporate practice of the disciplines that the relationship with God becomes the most personal and when God does some deep changing within the person. We can't say that is the only time God changes us because we can't limit when God will work within us.

Given the importance of the person's personal practice, there is a different way we need to see the role of the persons we have called "teachers in the church school" in the past. A better title is "guide." They will still be doing teaching but it will be more helpful to see them as guiding the children, youth and adults in the Christian journey. Guiding would involve becoming knowledgeable about persons' spiritual life and what they need in helping with it. It would involve encouraging them in their personal practices as well as talking with them personally about how their practices can be more helpful to them.

It is simply fundamental that people stop in their daily routine and pray on a regular basis in a way that is best for them. There are many ways we can connect with the Spirit speaking within us and a part of guidance is facilitating the learning of those ways, seeing to the practicing of them with others and then encouraging the doing of them in private. The objective then of guidance is to help the person come to practice a more receptive or contemplative way of being with God and therefore with each other. That includes one growing in being in touch with oneself and therefore with God, seeing the world from God's perspective, accepting the mystery and paradox in life, coming to life comfortably in the present moment with awareness.

The guidance process would also include guiding the private or group practice of "good works" or servanthood. Unless we experience what it means to be a servant we will not fully come to the inner experience of fulfillment that God calls us toward. Being in loving service, when it is truly done from the outpouring of love, even imperfectly, provides us with the confirmation of what it means to be a servant of God and a follower of Jesus.

The guidance of persons in their personal practice of the spiritual disciplines, privately and corporately, will be one of the more daunting tasks since we cannot control what anyone does. It will mean establishing some form of nonthreatening and supportive accountability for practicing the disciplines which usually best comes with folks being in a group where all are seeking to grow in their practice together. This can also happen, of course, in one-on-one spiritual direction or in group spiritual direction. A challenge may be in helping it happen in one of the ongoing groups who normally engage in study together.

In corporate worship our guidance is simply the way that we design the worship experience itself so that the person can in some way be helped to touch or be touched by the Sacred. That touch happens as we experience ourselves as a part of a loving community joined by God's Spirit. It happens as the scriptures are seen as truly relevant to our lives, as we say a sincere word of thanks and praise to God through a hymn or a prayer. It happens as we participate in receiving and tasting the love of God in the Lord's Supper and in hearing our oneness with others as we pray together for our needs. It happens when we hear the call to servanthood and find ourselves sent out with others to be followers of Jesus in the world. Corporate worship then can be a multi-sensory experience and a fundamental element in Christian nurture.

It may be obvious to some, but it needs to be made explicit that Guides in Christian nurture need to be on their own intentional spiritual journey. How can we guide another without our own experience in the journey? We will look at this further in the section on leadership in Part 3.

Teaching Processes

The second component is the arena of teaching processes and theories, of skills and methodologies to facilitate understanding, attitudes and skills by the individual and groups. When I have spoken of the problem with "schooling," it has been related to our learning about the Bible, theology, etc., for ourselves, believing that a person's beliefs was the goal. Education, in its broader theoretical meaning, has always included the inner life of the person, the maturing of the whole person. It is just that we in the church have tended to leave out the person's personal relationship with God and what nurtures that in what we have called education. That is why I have found it important to separate the two arenas for our purpose. This arena of learning—of understanding, attitudes and skills—is of tremendous importance for the preparation and support for the inner processes as well as for the task of servanthood. We have to have learning going on; it will be going on all the time anyway in some form so we must make it effective for our task.

Before going further it might be helpful to discuss the relationship between what we call teaching and the inner change of conversion. By teaching I mean the facilitating of a change in our understanding, attitudes and skills related to our living that helps us to adapt to the world around us and make greater sense of our place in it. In my way of understanding Christian maturation, conversion is fundamentally a change in the orientation of our spirit, our self-image, as it comes about through a growing relationship with God. This is what I tried to detail in the section on inner dynamics above. What teaching within the Christian context does then is to provide the source of understandings, attitudes and skills that support or make more possible the inner conversion toward which God is moving us. Just learning what is taught does not mean that we have necessarily made an inner spiritual change. The inner change requires our relationship with God for it to finally take place. We must admit that we, as guides or as teachers, may not be at all responsible for helping that relationship to take place in others when and where it does—we can only seek to be helpers as that becomes possible. The process of guidance and of teaching then are intertwined in actual nurture practice, but it is important to see them separately here to understand fully what we are about.

Let's start by using a simplified way of looking at the teaching processes in two basic approaches: the approach that starts with the content and the approach that starts with the learner.

In the content centered approach, the task is to simply help the person to learn a certain body of knowledge and to do so by using the methods and skills that best facilitate that kind of learning. In this approach you start with the content and you may tailor how you approach it with some regard to who the learners are and how they best learn, but you are first after teaching them a certain body of content. There are certain times within Christian nurture that such an approach may be helpful. For instance, when you are training persons to do a certain job on a mission experience, you will start with what they need to know to do the job. There may be times when you want to communicate certain knowledge about the Bible, for instance, when you are asking them to teach it to someone else. Content centered experiences are best when the persons are coming to learn what you are offering because they want it and know they need it. For the most part, however, this approach does not facilitate the inner growth as well as the second approach, so it will not be the one that should be used most in our nurture experiences even though we think that is the way we should do it.

In the person centered approach you start with the needs of the individuals involved. Even when you are dealing with a specific passage of scripture, how you approach it will be shaped by the person's life situation and needs. Within this approach there are two kinds of directions in designing nurture experiences: the direction in which there is a body of content that we need to communicate and the one in which we are focused only on the interests and needs of the individuals. In the first, we may be, for instance, wanting to study the Gospels over the next six months. In designing the sessions we will seek to understand the spiritual and life needs of the persons and deal with the content considering those needs so that we will have the greatest impact on facilitating those persons' inner growth. In the direction of designing with the focus only on the needs, you will choose the content that will be most relevant to the lives of those persons at that point. In deciding what to offer to adults, for instance, in the next planning cycle you will look to what kinds of issues they are facing in their lives and what is happening in the world that affects them. Why? Because that will make it more effective in helping them make the inner movement.

People are continually seeking meaning or significance for their lives as we said in the theology section. The Christian message provides a way to find that meaning and as we structure nurture experiences around their searching, we will be better able to help them find the true source of meaning in God. In addition, tailoring the content to their needs is a way of showing love because they see that the church is paying attention to where they are and affirming them where they are. It is another way in which we help them to come to see God as unconditionally loving.

There is an old piece of advice I learned early in my ministry that the teachable moment is the point at which the message of the Gospel intersects the life situation of the individual or group. What we are doing then is coming to know where our people are and what they are seeking and provide a way for them to explore how the Christian message is relevant to their life concerns.

To summarize, the best experiences for spiritual formation and learning are those that are sensitive to the life situation and developmental needs of the persons involved and relate the content to those needs. What we are about in our teaching, whichever approach seems best at the moment, is facilitating persons' inner change and their learning the ways of loving servanthood.

Factors in Teaching/Learning

Another aspect in the nurture process is to begin to understand some of the factors in what makes an experience an effective nurture experience from the view of teaching/learning. Here we will simply mention the factors and provide details in a later section.

Developmental Stage

One of the most important factors is the developmental stage of the individuals involved; is what we do "developmentally appropriate" to the people's lives. This is one of the ways that we tailor the experience to the person's needs. The developmental stages include cognitive, moral, psychosocial, and physical. We have to choose the content and the experiences that "fit" the people's stage of development so that they will have the most meaningful and effective experience possible. For instance, we cannot use concepts or biblical passages with children that are beyond their ability to understand or that will not be relevant to their life.

Multiple Intelligences

Each person has a preferred way he or she learns and it is built in. Some are more visual learners, some learn better through listening, etc. It will be important to provide different types of experiences to better meet the different learning styles.

Relational Climate

When persons feel emotionally safe, able to share freely and if the leader creates an atmosphere of openness and warmth, there is a greater level of openness to change and growth.

Physical Climate

The physical conditions of the location can also affect a person's openness. When the room is too cold or too hot people are distracted and not able to be as attentive to what is happening. The space should be inviting without noise interference from outside.

Leadership

It should go without saying that the ability and skill of the leader or facilitator greatly affects the learning potential of the experience. Does the leader know something about group dynamics, about asking questions, about choices in and use of methodologies?

Methodology

The activities used by the leader in the experience will affect how well the person learns and changes. Lecture is found to be the least effective method through which persons learn although for some purposes and settings it may be the best choice. Young children learn best through a center approach and through play. Every experience should have some way of interacting with the content and a time for sharing. The section below on key experiences is a way of looking at basic methodology. We will discuss methods in more detail in a later section.

CHAPTER 4

KEY NURTURE EXPERIENCES

In the section on the nature of faith we discussed the three faculties as a way of talking about the aspects of our personhood that help us to understand what must be involved in nurture experiences for us to reach the whole person and thereby be more effective. As we seek to enable and facilitate the person's relationship with God and becoming a loving person, there are certain types of experience that are central to the processes that accomplish the engaging of the faculties of Intellect, Spirit and Will—the whole person—which must happen in order for our efforts to bear fruit. In the process of design at the more detailed levels we must consider our use of these various key experiences. I introduce them here as some of the more basic and practical parts of a formation perspective. (These experiences are also referred to in Chapter 8 in the section on planning specific nurture experiences.)

The concept of the key experiences that are central to nurture took root with me a long time ago in learning what constitutes an effective Sunday School session. To engage the whole person it is not enough to talk simply about study, worship, fellowship and service. These types of experiences, described below, embody many if not all the processes discussed in the various approaches written about in recent books on Christian education. You might call these the categories that contain various methodologies used to fulfill the experience because they are the vehicles for both the inner and the outward journey.

The key experiences and their associated methods are the carriers for the nurture experience. These modes should be considered in planning intentional nurture experiences, which would include both a specific session for Sunday morning or other times or to some degree in designing the year long "curriculum" for a specific age level ministry. The point is that these experiences must be present for persons to have all of their faculties engaged so that their formation is fully enabled and we accoplish our task in the best possible way. These key experiences are:

Awareness
Expression
Information Communication
Interaction/Interpretation
Practice/Action-Reflection
Sharing
Committing

The following is a description of these experiences and how they relate to the three faculties:

1. **Awareness** involves experiences in which persons would become aware of what is going on within them, what they are feeling, what they feel they need, what they know already about a topic and what experiences they have already had. This is crucial so that in sharing persons receive respect and attention for who they are, and also it sets the stage for the integration of whatever new will next be encountered. When another listens to us we have a greater sense of importance—our spirit is nurtured— and we become less afraid and thereby more open to what we will encounter next. When we feel strong in our spirit we feel more confident in receiving new information or experiences and more willing to integrate it with what we already know and who we already are. Bringing to consciousness what we know

is helpful in the intellectual processes of accommodation and/ or assimilation that must take place for us to grow and change. Theologically, as we become aware we are affirmed as children of God with our own God-given abilities and selfhood.

2. **Expression** This type of experience is related to awareness, but I include it because it comprises those times when the love we feel within us comes out and we want to express our thankfulness or our love of God or another person. It refers to the times when we just want to do something that we enjoy for the sheer sake of enjoying it—times of "play"! It may involve creating a work of art as an expression of joy or even sorrow. It may involve saying thank you to others for just being who they are. These experiences may be times of worship or recreation. They may be quiet reflective times—and here they are related to awareness. We must help people to take the time to express who they are in creative, freeing ways. We must also help people to know how to worship in ways that truly express their thankfulness and their relationship with God. Expressive times are chances for us to let our Spirit out in celebration of life.

3. **Information Communication** is the experience that we have basically sought to perform in the church school when we provide some form of information, concepts, beliefs, etc., that relate to the meaning of the gospel for the person's life or provide them with the values and practices that enable them to be loving in the world. The providing of such input is crucial, but it must be done in a way most conducive to persons receiving it and integrating it into their lives, which involves using some of the other modes of experience along with the information input. This information communication relates to the intellectual faculty, of course, and provides persons with concepts and language with which to name the experiences they have had or understand the experiences they will encounter. The information persons need will help them to build their spirit and shape their Will. Information input will be woven into almost all the experiences in some form including training

sessions about practices or skills. Story telling has become one of the more important techniques in information communication. To tell a story does more than just provide intellectual content because it also can communicate emotion and tradition that are so important to a Christian perspective.

4. **Interaction/Interpretation** Interaction is that experience that is necessary to help us to process the information we receive so we can integrate it into our living. One could also call the experience one of "interpretation." It is the experience in which persons come to grips with what the concept or experience they have had means for their lives, how it fits into the tapestry of their existence. It is an active experience involving questioning, hands on kinds of working with the ideas, reflecting on their experiences, practicing the behaviors they have learned are helpful. In the group we might use art, writing, role play, or other activities along with questions and discussion. I suppose we can say that interaction happens throughout our daily living as we take what we have heard or read and try it out in some way or another. Interaction within the intentional formational experience is the most helpful to the individual because there we can provide guidance in reflection upon the interaction. The serendipity interaction in life can be used by bringing it into the intentional experience. Interaction facilitates the intellectual faculty in placing the concepts in place with other concepts we hold. As conceptual integration takes place there is also an integration within the Spirit as an idea is related to how persons see themselves as well as others. In interaction persons are able to see how a certain action or idea affects them or others and therefore it shapes the Will.

5. **Practicing/Action-Reflection** could be seen as a form of interaction as we discussed in #4 above, but I am putting it separately to make it very obvious. Practice can be staged or it can be just what happens in life between intentional nurture experiences. When I say practice I am thinking of actually taking our folks outside the church and letting them practice

being loving in the world through various kinds of service projects or even interactive experiences with other people. It can also be within the church walls as well as we involve our people in learning prayer forms, planning and leading worship, leading groups themselves, etc. The big difference in this kind of experience when it is intentionally formational is that the persons involved are also called upon together to talk about their thinking and feeling and intending as they went though the experience. Such a sharing does not often happen in the daily run of living. This mode is involved in what has been called the "action/reflection model."

6. **Sharing** is fully an interpersonal process in difference from interaction, which is often a more individual experience, though not necessarily so. Sharing's central function is to work with the Spirit faculty as persons share what they have experienced and gain some feedback about whether or not they are still acceptable to the universe. This is why in sharing it is not helpful for someone listening to another's sharing to start giving advice. We rather need to help people to think through and come to know what they are feeling about the experience and to find acceptance for their feelings and their experience. Certainly there are critical times when some one is actually asking for help with something, but the group can learn to know the difference and how to respond. Such sharing is at the heart of spiritual direction, whether one-on-one or in a group. It is absolutely essential that people have the opportunity to share about their relationship with God so that the Loving Community can provide the context and support the needs in those darker times on the spiritual journey. Sharing about the other kinds of experiences, say after an interaction experience, persons are again allowed to share from their Spirit as an affirming as well as integrating process. In sharing difficult times, or in a time of confessing, the process is especially one in which there is the great need to find support and love so that the Spirit can be affirmed even though they have done an unloving thing. It

is when we are affirmed in the midst of our unloving actions that our spirit comes to truly feel the unconditional love of God. Sharing is an important part of our intellectual processes of assimilation and accommodation as we work on putting a new concept into its proper place in our understanding of life. Sharing is community building; it creates ties between those who share. It is very important to learn methods to intentionally build community at the beginning of a group's life.

7. **Committing** is fundamentally a process that provides the opportunity for the person to shape the Will. Times of commitment, however small or great, are times when people decide to shape their Will a certain way, or at least are able to confirm in the community the shape their Will has already taken. It is in times of commitment that persons in a more profound way are called to state who they truly are and affirm their value orientation and actually come to a deeper realization of who they are and what they want in life where it was not that clear up to that time. Of course, the call to commitment must be done in a non-coercive way and should grow out of the experiences of people and follow naturally the flow of their lives. This is why the church should consider developing more rituals that enable commitment and confirmations at many different points in our lives.

You will most likely be using these types of experiences already in various ways, without knowing what or why. They may seem like they would be simply methods, but they are more foundational in that they must be included in an overall design whereas a particular "method" may not be. Also, a method would be the way in which one of these key experiences is carried out. The key experiences are also suggestive of experiences that you may or may not think to consider otherwise. For instance, the experience of "committing" suggests that you plan specific times within the worship service or elsewhere in which persons can make a personal commitment to a way of servanthood at a particular point in their lives. Confirmation is, of course, the prime example, but there should be more times set aside when people go on mission trips or when they take on a certain task as a part of the church's ministry. It is important that we become more aware of the kinds of experiences we offer and why, so that our efforts will be more effective.

PART 2

THE TASK OF
CHRISTIAN NURTURE

This part has two sections. We have looked at the theology, the inner dynamics and the nurture processes; now we must try to lay out how that takes shape in the task of Christian nurture. First we will look at a possible description of the task beginning with a vision of what we hope will be the outcome in the lives of our people. We will lay out a description following a proposed objective with two parts that focus on the inward and the outward journeys of the spiritual life. It is necessary for the limited purpose of this writing to make the description of the task brief. There is, of course, much detail to be worked out to put this fully into practice, but that is not my purpose here.

The second section looks at some issues in the context of the local church where nurture will take place and suggests some directions that need to be taken. The home and the local congregation are the heart of ongoing nurture of Christians. The actual majority of spiritual nurture takes place (or is hindered) in the home, but what happens in the local church is of central importance to shape what happens in the home and elsewhere. It is with the local church setting, then, that this writing is most focused.

CHAPTER 5

NURTURE IN THE SACRED RHYTHM

Our task in this chapter is to define the task of Christian nurture in functional terms and that function is characterized in the term, "the Sacred Rhythm" which refers to a way of understanding the Christian journey and life. We will propose a vision and then an objective guided by our Rhythm, followed by a more detailed description of the task as shaped by the Rhythm.

A Vision and Objective

I choose to use the vision that I find in the scriptures about the ultimate coming of the Kingdom of God on Earth--a vision of a world where God's peace and justice prevails for all creation and all of God's family, here and now, in our history. The way God's Kingdom will come about is through our participation with God as God's servants in the image of Jesus. We are disciples, followers and learners, certainly, but our task is one of servanthood in bringing about God's dream for creation.

If servants of God in Christ is our goal, the result of our efforts, what will it take to nurture servants of God's Kingdom? Following our theological foundations it is fundamental that if one is to be a servant of God, then one would be in a relationship with God from which one would receive the power to be a servant. It is God's love, remember, that frees us and calls us, then energizes us for the servant task. Second, then, we would have to know something about what it means to be servants, what it means to be loving and some skills necessary for the task. These are the two great movements of one's spiritual life, of someone on the journey with God. I call these movements the "Sacred Rhythm" of life: The movement toward openness to God, to receiving God's love (the Sabbath movement) and our movement outward to service in the world (the Servanthood movement). The movement inward is essential to empower the movement out to serve the world for God. The movement outward drives us back deeper into our relationship with God and moves us toward fulfilling God's call to bring about the Kingdom in our world. Besides seeing this in Wesley's General Rules, it can be seen in the Great Commandment to love God and to love your neighbor as yourself. I find it in the quote in the Introduction from Thomas Kelly--upon God's catching us depends the history of the world. Through guiding persons in this Sacred Rhythm we facilitate the movements of the inner dynamic and accomplish our task through God's grace.

If we take this basic rhythm as the model for the Christian life of servanthood, then we can form a two-part objective for Christian nurture:

> *To help the person to enter and nurture a personal relationship with God in Christ*
> and
> *To help the person to know what it means to be a loving servant in the world and to go about serving.*

About the wording of this objective: The words *"To help …"* are carefully chosen. Do we truly accept the idea that God is the one who transforms us, and that it is not we who bring the transformation? Do we accept that persons are actually in control of how they respond to God or not? If we do, then we see ourselves as "helpers" of God's movements. Such an acceptance will make a tremendous difference in how we approach our task. The words "to help" are fundamental to the objective statement.

Such an objective, as simple as it is, is both focused on what is needed and is also functional. It tells us the outcome we want and gives us a direction for process. I believe that one of the most needed aspects of our leadership development is to help persons to know what it is they are called to accomplish and why that is important. Usually we just give them the curriculum resources and say, "go teach." That leaves them with no real way to be creative with their own insights and understandings of the faith. So we need a way to clearly talk about what we are trying to do and such an objective will enable us to do so.

What is involved in fulfilling this objective? In the first, the inward movement, the focus is on persons participating in the spiritual disciplines and coming to nurture their own personal relationship with God. That focus is guided by Biblical study, by teaching about the disciplines, coming to understand the unconditionally loving nature of God and Jesus, and learning to share our faith with others; all within the traditions and practices of the supportive loving community who worships and prays together.

In the outward movement the focus is on the person becoming involved in being a servant. That focus is guided by Biblical study, by the teachings of Jesus and the way of love, by learning what it means to love in all of our life situations and what God has to do with our loving, actually experiencing service in a learning situation and being encouraged to be aware and commit to our own personal calling— again, all within the life of the community that is going out to serve the world.

The point I want to drive home is that in both movements there is both the educational and the inner formational components that are integrated to form an effective whole as a ministry. This is what I believe will make the difference in our ministry of nurture and is what we must, in some form, bring about!

We will look next in more detail at the two journeys pointed to above.

Reflect

Certainly the wording of the above objective is only one way to say it. You must work out what you will use to guide your ministry. Can you state now what you might say is an objective that states it more helpfully in your view?

The Sacred Rhythm as a Structure for Nurture

We need to say more about what goes into the two elements of our objective as a way of further describing what an intentional nurture effort is like when seen as the movements of the Sacred Rhythm.

The Journey into God's Love

The journey into a relationship with God is a journey into God's love toward the full acceptance of that love. The practice of the spiritual disciplines is central to that journey and the facilitation of the person's practices is the central task of Christian nurture. The journey inward is central, as I have been trying to say, because one's acceptance of God's love is fundamental to one's conversion. Surrender to God's love overcomes the fear and frees us to be all we are created to be and to love others.

Let's now sort out the elements in the nurture practices involved in our facilitation of this inner journey. (Some of this will have been mentioned in the theological section.) To do that we will start with those experiences that facilitate the spiritual disciplines in the life of the individual. The list of disciplines we will use for our purpose here includes personal prayer, corporate prayer (worship, including especially the sacraments), reading and study of the Scriptures, acts of letting go, and sharing love in the Christian community. (This list is taken from Wesley's General rules in the section on the "ordinances of God" and you may have a different way of listing them.) What will go into our helping the person to know these disciplines and really use them effectively? Note that in presenting this I am foregoing a discussion of the ways nurture is best done in the different age groups; that comes later. Here is an overview to try to communicate the "big picture."

The most basic nurture effort is to show our people that they are loved by our actions. This effort is also basic to the person entering a relationship with God because who wants to have a relationship with One who only cares about us if we do the "right thing" or who is judgmental and arbitrary? Showing them they are loved includes how we greet them and show them they are important, by offering experiences that fit their age and stage of development and life situation and any way that they know they are a part of the community. These actions are a part of helping them to feel that God loves them because they associate the Christian community with God. For young children this is especially true and certainly their Sunday school teacher is a stand-in for God.

Then comes teaching them that they are loved by God in any way we can, beginning of course with the Bible and with stories of Jesus. How we handle the biblical content is critical as we seek to communicate God as a God of unconditional love so it will take our focused effort. (See the section on the Bible and nurture later in the book)

And in teaching the biblical perspective we also communicate some very basic theological concepts in appropriate ways. We can help them to understand how God works in a relationship with God, that God is within them, loving them and trying to help them with their lives. Teaching that they are loved also means saying something about our own created goodness, that we are loved just as we are and so is everyone else.

Along with this basic orientation to God's love, we will be teaching them the ways of personal prayer and helping them to begin to practice it as appropriate to their age and stage. We show them how in a group and then encourage them to do it at home and help them share about their experiences in practicing it. I believe that teaching the way of silent and receptive prayer is fundamental. The relationship with God is one, as we have said, of learning to allow God to love us so that we come to trust it and know it intimately.

We will be teaching them the ways of corporate prayer or worship. So many of us do not know how to worship, the meaning of the rituals, of the Lord's Supper, of the seasonal observances. This understanding needs to be passed on early and in a setting outside of the worship service as well as within it. Corporate worship can involve the senses--the visual and the physical and the auditory--and be a powerful communication of the Faith's Story and of God's love. The worship service is the key context of how the whole church nurtures persons in the faith--when it is done with intention to nurture and not just to proclaim and certainly not to entertain.

The study of the Bible is a central element in nurture, but it is only effective for our journey inward when its focus is on the person's relationship with God. This does not mean that we will not study the scriptures in depth but then when we do, it is done to understand what it means for our relationship with God. We will teach the stories of the faith as stories and delve into them to help the person understand the loving nature of God and how God calls us to respond to that love. The stories can be even more meaningful, however, when we go behind them to understand when and why they were written and by whom using the latest in biblical scholarship. Studying the Bible also has the effect of enriching our personal prayer. As we pray it is so important to be able to remember the words of scripture that affirm God's love for us—it is one way that God speaks to us in prayer. Also, there are forms of praying with the scriptures that can be very helpful to know and learn to use.

Acts of Letting Go—my words to replace Wesley's "fasting and abstinence" to interpret them for today's world. Certainly fasting is still practiced by many people and is a valid discipline that can be helpful when rightly understood. I believe that fasting and abstinence refer to the deeper willingness on our part to give up whatever stands in the way of our greater dependence on God. We are called to give up those things that we depend upon for meaning rather than depending on God. Fasting can be a reminder for us to give up those other things in our lives, but we can also seek, with God's help, to actually give up what we hold as little gods in our lives. This arena of teaching and practice relates directly to the second movement discussed in the formational dynamics section. We must help people to know what it is that can and does stand in the way of a deeper relationship with God and then know how in our prayer to let go of those dependencies so that the letting go actually takes place in our lives.

Sharing in the community refers to several ways in which we depend upon the community for our nurture. The Christian life is not an individual affair but a community one. We need others to help us when we can't touch God on our own. It is important for persons to be helped to see the gift of depending on others. That can begin by simply doing more sharing about our spiritual life with others in the nurture groups--which we don't do enough of at all. It can be very important to simply keep up with people and help them know they are an important part of the community and their presence is needed for another's upbuilding. The use of small groups for spiritual growth experiences is very needed as a place where people can share about their prayer and their callings as well as their personal needs within a loving group. One-to-one spiritual guidance can be a very helpful ministry when offered by trained persons. That guidance can also be done in small groups and it can happen when we call on special friends when we need to share. What will be critical here is that we teach persons how to seek and share help about our relationship with God, which goes so much further than simply sharing at the emotional level, though that is also important.

The Journey Outward to the World

Our task is growing up servants of God's justice and peace and the way to that must go through nurturing persons in their personal relationship with God to know they are loved, but it does not stop there. We are created to be loving, but we are not born knowing how to love. The relationship with God, receiving God's love, overcomes our fear and the barriers to be loving; the further task then is to help persons to know how to love in all the situations and at all the stages in their lives.

There are at least three facets of the nurture of the person in this journey outward. The first is simply teaching the ways of love at the heart of Christianity. Then there is the involvement of the person in actual servant experiences. Third is the providing of opportunities for persons to discern their callings, make public commitments to those callings and then to be celebrated in the community for their servanthood.

Teaching the ways of love certainly involves the biblical teachings of the Commandments, of Jesus' teachings and examples and Paul's words about living out the Gospel. We would include the many helpful writings of the saints of Christian history and especially those of our most recent history. There is much we can look to for help in what to teach. It will be necessary to not only teach what we are to do, but to look at our present society and become aware of the situations that need our prophetic words and servant activities. It is too easy for our people to be seduced by our culture and not see the way in which the church must stand against various aspects of the culture if we are to be truly concerned to help God bring about God's reign in our world.

Taking persons on servanthood experiences is a common occurrence and we know a lot about doing it. One common mistake, however, is not seeing them also as nurture experiences. To do so means that we provide time for reflection and prayer about our experiences, before, during and after. The persons who go are not always mature in their spirit and they need the connection with God as a part of the experience. Remember that doing good and doing no harm are a part of the spiritual disciplines set out by Wesley, but servanthood experiences can only be such a discipline as they are connected to our relationship with God and put in the proper perspective as a way in which we both allow God's love to flow through us to others and allow God's love to reach us through those we serve.

Finally, a person's recognition of his/her calling and a chance to make that commitment in the community is of great importance. We too often miss asking persons to think about what it is that God is calling them to and teaching that the call is already within them ready to be discerned through their prayer and in conversation with others.

So many of our people are already following their calling and need to be recognized by the community, possibly through some annual ritual in worship. Then there should be a time when persons who have realized a calling can make a public commitment before the congregation as a way of being affirmed and supported.

There are, of course, many more details to be discussed in each of these movements, some of which will be touched on in what follows, but all cannot be covered in this work. It is important to see these movements in relationship to the overall ministry design of the congregation. Some of the content of the nurture experiences will be provided by what else is happening, such as the seasonal celebrations in worship or mission focused experiences. Other parts will be designed specifically within the nurture experiences for the age groups and special opportunities. We must not, however, allow the larger special experiences to keep us from paying attention to the details of what happens in the nurture experiences that contribute to greater effectiveness. Often we think that just doing a greater number of special events is accomplishing something when it is not. The effectiveness will be over the long run, in the loving relationships between persons, in how well the experience is carried out, and in the way the content nurtures persons' relationship with God or shows them what it means to be loving.

Just so we can be clear about what I am proposing, let me repeat what I have said about the heart of the transition from the past to the future. The issue is the relationship of education and formation and how we see what we are trying to accomplish in Christian nurture because it has everything to do with how effectively we nurture our people. Education, defined here as the communication of knowledge about subjects important to the life of a Christian, will always be critical in a nurture ministry. What will be essential for the future is the additional and central importance of what we call spiritual formation, the nurturing of the person's inner, personal relationship with God. It is not that we did not think that the inner growth was important; it is just that we had never learned what it meant for our efforts at nurture and how that inner growth comes about. Right now, these two facets of nurture, education and spiritual formation are too often seen as separate efforts, but they must be integrated. The information we pass on should be so structured as to aid in the spiritual formation of the individual, and the formational experiences must be guided by the faithful understanding of the tradition. What happens in each nurture session should seek to be a melding of the two so that in all cases the person's relationship with God as well as his/her call to servanthood is our objective.

CHAPTER 6

NURTURE IN THE LOCAL CHURCH

We have outlined the future task of Christian nurture for the contemporary church. How then will that task be carried out? We must foster the processes by which Christian nurture occurs in two places: the home and the local Christian community. Whatever else happens in the home, the community or beyond ultimately depends upon local Christian communities and how they nurture Christians.

Taking Responsibility for Nurture Effectiveness

What happens in Christian nurture happens most intensively in the local congregation, whether that is a denominational group, a house church or a monastic community. When that local group is the "beloved community" then the people in it are most likely to see themselves as the people of God and become servants of God.

All local churches are doing something in the way of nurture, the only issue being whether it is effective. I have proposed that the fundamental lack of effectiveness has to do with how we see the task of Christian nurture, the vision of which I have tried to outline above. The next hurdle then is our leadership knowing how to perform the task effectively. We have looked briefly at the state of support and the lack of it for nurture ministry from beyond the local church which would certainly have a great deal to do with any lack of effectiveness in the local church. It is not at all clear how we will move at the Annual Conference or General church levels to rebuild any beyond the local church support for the local ministries and even what that would look like given the present climate in the Church. I do believe that there must be a commitment to create some form of support for the local church beyond what we are now doing, whatever shape of a nurture ministry we propose to use.

Which brings us to the local church's commitment to intentional nurture as an essential ministry of the congregation in its own right. Let's be positive and say that the congregation truly is concerned about nurture; then the issue is one of seeing the need to do something differently and knowing how to do it. What is the source of any communication and support for the congregation to know what and how? As long as there is a vacuum from beyond the local church, the congregation has to step up to the plate and become more intentional about what it does and be willing to provide the resources and leadership to get the job done. This means that the local church has to become more responsible for its nurture ministry and not depend simply on some program purchased from wherever because it sounds interesting. The congregation in one sense has to come to know how to design its own curriculum and find or create the needed resources. That will take some help from outside the congregation, but it may take congregations prevailing upon the annual conference to begin to provide that help along with using the help available from the General Board of Discipleship, most of which will be online. The local church asking for it, however, depends upon the congregation believing that it needs the help.

The local church is the incarnation of God's love when it is serving faithfully and therefore is the point at which the Kingdom becomes more of a reality in the world. For that to truly be the case, the members of the congregation must be growing in their faith, in their relationship with God, which is what nurture is all about. Are we willing to truly commit to the task?

The Whole Church Nurtures

Our approach to nurture in this book is that it is an essential element in the church's ministry alongside of worship, missions, etc. At the same time we know that people are nurtured in the faith in some way, positively or negatively, by all that happens in a congregation. That means that all ministries must take seriously what they are doing so that they are nurturing in a way that is effective and helps people toward the objectives. Given that the nurture task demands some level of understanding of what it takes to effectively nurture people in the faith, this overarching reality may be more difficult for some congregations to manage, though not impossible.

It may be helpful to look at our task as involving both overall ministry design to which nurture experiences provide support and intentional nurture experiences based on what persons need to know about the Gospel and how it relates to their lives. A congregation may decide, for instance, that during Eastertide it wants to focus on the issues of family life. That means worship content would deal with those issues, but specific nurture experiences, whether within the Sunday schedule or outside of it or both, would also provide courses, classes, seminars, retreats or whatever is needed. We will look at this again in the section on design.

A very powerful nurturing element in the congregation is worship because it reaches more people and has more potential impact. Worship can provide visual, auditory, and sensory experiences that can be wonderfully effective in communicating thoughts as well as engendering inner experiences that are truly growing experiences. Worship and nurture are after the very same objectives although through different contexts and experiences. Unfortunately, not all worship services are designed to be as effective for nurture as is their potential because they usually are not planned with nurture in mind. The deficit in worship, however, is that it does not provide the in depth personal sharing that is needed, so our worship must be wedded to our intentional nurture efforts at other times.

The second most powerful nurture experience in the congregation, outside of the specific nurture ministry, is that of mission outreach or servant opportunities. It will be very important to plan servant experiences in cooperation with the ongoing nurture opportunities for the age levels and include those aspects that make intentional nurture possible.

Administrative sessions can also become nurture as well as training experiences for leadership. What happens when we plan for ministry is critical for the results of our planning but also can be a spiritually deepening experience for the group members if we intentionally plan for that outcome.

What happens in the specific nurture ministry and what happens elsewhere in the congregation need some intentional cooperative planning so that the opportunity for positive nurture experiences is optimized in all arenas.

Working Across Ministry Lines

What is said above about the whole congregation nurturing calls for staff members and lay leaders to lay aside any sense of ownership they might feel about their particular area of ministry and work with each other. It will take the pastor and worship planners for instance to be willing to ask for ideas about nurture from persons who are trained in that task. It will call for those in specific nurture ministries to have their plans open to being integrated with what is happening in the larger congregation.

It would be a grand day when pastors are expected to receive some training in the education and formation processes so that they will know how to plan more effectively. I would hope that someday seminaries will see the importance of returning the nurture ministries to their rightful place in the required curriculum.

Whether that time comes or not it will be critical for the local church leadership to be open to help from other reliable sources, not to be told what their ministry must be like but to receive the skills and understandings to be able to plan what is the most effective ministry for their congregation.

Characteristics of the Local Ministry

A Focus on the Home

The Church has waxed hot and cold in its emphasis on Christian nurture in the home. We have never forgotten it entirely, but we don't do much to support it except for those local instances where it is of more importance. It has always been the case that the very small amount of time that the child or youth spends in some nurture experience in the church is no match for the time spent in the home or community outside the church. We must have the support of nurture in the home to be effective in our nurture as a congregation. Nurture in the home actually begins by nurturing the adults who are parents and grandparents. That means that one of the key focuses of nurture in the future must be on supporting and training the parents and grandparents who will be doing that nurturing. Adult education focused on the home environment should take a top priority in our local churches.

It has been too easy for this writer to not see this issue as important as it is and I imagine that will go for many us. We have been so focused on whether the church institution is maintained that we have forgotten about the future that is lodged in the nurture of our children and youth. We have been obsessed with providing an at least inviting ministry for children and youth in the church and forgotten where they spend most of their time. I am certainly not belittling the necessity of the efforts that take place within the church community; they are crucial. I am just pointing out that we are missing a great arena of nurture when we forget the home. Can we then begin to make the home a true focus by providing support and training for our parents in nurturing Faith in their homes?

Going Deep, Broad and Long Range

It is our usual perspective to just see that we have a Sunday School for the different ages and some additional events at other times to nurture our people. It is time we begin to look deeper, broader, and for the long haul as we plan for those times as well as our whole ministry. To look deeper means to seek to be more relevant to the lives of our people and to help them to look deeply at their own spiritual growth. To be broad is to be sure we serve folks at all stages in their journey. To be long range is to plan for folks in the full span of their lives.

Going Deep: People are hungry for a touch of the sacred and we have too long shied from helping them to find it, so that now they are too afraid of it to say they want it or they don't know that that is what they want. We have too often provided them with a superficial spirituality that entertains but does not really satisfy. We have tried to sell them a "self-help" version of Christianity that is more salvation by works than salvation by grace, which has left them no better off. They have not come to know the more difficult but tremendously satisfying spiritual journey of truly surrendering to God's work in their lives which I believe is one of the main reasons we have lost members. Our task now is to help them to receive that touch of the Sacred, of God, of Christ in a way that truly helps them in their lives. When our people face tragedy, illness, just the daily difficulties of living, their relationship with God needs to mean something to them. In today's world so many people cannot find that relationship through some of the traditional images and practices. It will take our helping them explore ways that go back beyond the traditional as well as into the future images that are being expressed.

Going Broad: There is a great need to pay attention to the stages of the spiritual journey or the various levels of spiritual maturity in our congregations. People at different stages need different kinds of help. There are folks who have had a bad experience in the church in the past but are still searching for a meaningful way to God. There are people who are still afraid they are not acceptable to God, as well as those who are well into their spiritual journey. We also have a major problem of biblical and theological illiteracy. People just don't know much about the Bible or the Christian tradition, and they may not want to learn because they see no relevancy in learning (which gets us back to going deeper). One of the critical arenas is that of those folks who grew up and were nurtured deeply in the faith and who have served broadly in the life of the church and are asking, "Well, what more is there for me?" They are asking because they need to be helped to go deeper not just serve more.

Going Long Range: Nurturing people in the Faith needs to begin the moment they are born and continue until they breathe their last breath. How well do we know how to help the infant feel God's love and help the dying adults know their lives are held by God and so have meaning? Do we know how we can help those who struggle with the trials of adolescence or the new parent who needs to know how to relate to the child and the spouse, or the retiring businessman who has only found meaning in his work and now it will be gone? Much is being written now about the way the church must learn how to speak to the young adult as well as minister to the growing numbers of retiring adults. We cannot afford to forget the folks in between. What it takes is an intentional effort to design a ministry of nurture that touches all stages in a person's life. It is not just a matter of keeping people involved; it is more a matter of what they find in our congregations that is meaningful for their lives where they are. Just an interesting program, even if it seems to have some relevancy to it, will not answer the yearnings.

Focusing on the Task and Not the Program

It is very easy to see what we are doing as creating or maintaining a program structure such as the Sunday School or a small group ministry because we believe that such programs will do the job we want. Of course we have to have such programs, but in planning them do we first consider how we are to fulfill our ministry and not how we simply create or maintain this or that program? For instance, in seeking to nurture adults who are not coming to Sunday morning classes, do we simply mount a big effort to get them there or do we ask ourselves what other, and possibly more effective, means can we use to nurture their faith. Do we create internet options or a gathering at another time of the week. Churches are already trying some different options— maybe you are too—and the challenge will be to offer something that is truly nurturing or formative and not just entertaining. Another example is the pastor in a small church. He or she does not need to create a full Sunday school structure but instead think about how best to nurture folks in that situation with however many will come and wherever and whenever it can be done.

Doing What We Do Only Better AND/OR Really Changing What We Do

It may be that we need to do things differently in a big way in our local church, but it also may be that we just need to do what we do better than we are doing it. The critical issue I am pushing is our effectiveness in doing nurture and what goes into that effectiveness. Let's just ask ourselves whether what we are doing is truly effective in terms of quality nurture. Maybe we need to ask whether we know what quality nurture is, and what is truly effective.

The criteria for effectiveness in the religious/spiritual realm can be elusive, but we can come to know what works best when it comes to helping persons to learn what is truly helpful in nurturing a relationship with God. The scope of those things can be broad in some areas, but there are some criteria nevertheless. It is up to the local church to seek out that criteria of quality and effectiveness and get on with the task. It may be that when we look at the criteria we will find that we need to change a great deal. It will be a part of faithfulness to not resist that change but to embrace it.

CHAPTER 7

GUIDELINES FOR CHRISTIAN NURTURE

As we have said, this perspective on Christian Nurture is not a detailed program to be put in place and run. It is, instead, an approach, a way of going about growing committed Christians in your local congregation. The intention of this book is to provide you with some guidelines, suggestions, etc., that will help you provide the most effective nurture possible done in your unique way. The following content grows out of the previous sections but seeks to provide you with perceptual and structural ways of visualizing the implementation of Christian nurture. All that has gone before has sought to give you a description of the "stance," the attitudes and concerns with which we must go about nurture. Now we try to become more specific, at least as specific as we can and still provide you with the latitude to develop your ministry as fits your situation. In this section we will begin by revisiting the objectives of nurture and then move to the key focuses of our nurture efforts and the four arenas of nurture that we believe need to be in place in any congregation. Part Three provides some thoughts about the details of designing and implementation.

Using the Objectives

To remind us, our objectives are two:

> *To help persons to enter and nurture a personal relationship with God in Christ*
> and
> *To help them to know what it means to be a loving servant in the world and to go about serving.*

These two statements form the overall intention and direction of our efforts in nurture. If, in the future, we were to step back and look at what we have been doing in our nurture efforts, we would need to ask whether or not we have been meeting these two objectives whatever the details of the ministry have been. That is the purpose of these objectives: to give us a clear direction for action in all that we seek to do with the trust that in fulfilling them we will provide effective nurture or will understand why we did not accomplish that goal.

Is It Relevant to Our Objective?

Is what we decide to deal with in any of our nurture experiences relevant to the outcome we desire, and that God desires for our people? If you have worked out a meaningful guiding objective, will you follow its guidance, or will you simply plan what seems to be popular or available at the moment? I believe that everything we decide to offer must be looked at under the light of our objective, otherwise we cease to be effective. If the objective seems to get in the way, then we need to look at how our objective is structured. The point here is to plan and implement that which will move us toward where we need and want to be—to seek intentionally to be effective in our nurture.

Focuses of Nurture Content

The "focus" of nurture is another way to further concretize the actions that must be brought to our task if our nurture is to be effective.

In a sense, this is a way of summarizing all that has been offered in Parts One and Two as to what is important and what we can do to implement it. We are offering four focuses to guide our efforts: inner formation, traditioning, cultivating a prophetic stance, and servanthood. These are the areas that should form our efforts in our preaching, teaching and guiding in terms of content. They come from the theology and the spiritual dynamics that we have explored above. They are not a separate structure, but one axis of a matrix, if you will, that will help us be sure that we are "covering all the bases" in each of our efforts in terms of the content of what we are doing. Not that all of these will be evident in all experiences, but that if we looked at all of the experiences together there would be a balance of each one so that a focus is not being slighted or left out. A word about each one will be helpful to be sure of what is being communicated through these terms. (There will be some repetition of content from earlier sections, but hopefully that will be more helpful than a distraction.)

Focus 1: Inner Formation— The Journey into God's Love

In Parts One and Two you will certainly have found the stress on inner formation as the aspect that we have most neglected in our past efforts at nurture. Therefore, the development of this focus is of prime importance in our nurture efforts. You have read a more detailed presentation of this aspect in Chapter 5, so this is simply a review of what this focus would include in terms of the content of our teaching and guidance.

Fundamental to the inner formation efforts are, of course, the ways in which the congregational environment promotes a sense of unconditional love and acceptance to those who participate. This ranges from what is said in the sermons, to the greeters at the doors, to the way the Sunday School teachers relate to the individuals in their groups. It has to do with the way experiences are planned so that they are sensitive to the developmental stage and needs of the individuals both in terms of the intellectual content and the methods employed.

A focus on inner formation means the teaching of and the guidance of persons in their use of the spiritual disciplines so that they will be involved in nurturing their relationship with God away from as well as within the congregation. It is very important that our teaching and guidance help the person to learn what it means to pray a prayer of receptivity to God's love and a way of listening for God's guidance from within. It involves helping persons to become self aware of who they are as God's Beloved and to know how to listen for God's callings.

Inner formation certainly includes an ongoing guidance in the ways of corporate worship, of participation in the sacraments, etc.— ongoing because the way we perceive of such experiences changes with our developmental growth. The design of worship can also contribute greatly to inner transformation.

Remember that the way in which we use the Bible makes a great difference in whether inner formation is positive or not. The passages we choose make a great difference depending upon the age of the individual as to whether he or she develops a helpful or harmful understanding of the nature of God.

The ways we help persons to share about their spiritual life is of great importance since sharing provides us with affirmation as well as chance for self-expression. The use of small groups is critical in inner formation because of this opportunity to have more intimate relationships with others. How we share with others is directly related to our sharing with God.

Focus 2: Traditioning—The Language and the Ways of Being Christian

When we say "traditioning" we are talking about the socialization of persons into the Christian family. That means that they learn all that it means to be a Christian in terms of how we live together, the meaning of the language of Christianity, knowing the stories of the Faith, and the practices that show that we are Christian. To "tradition" is not to create someone who thinks that Christianity is better than other religions or the only religion, but simply to know who we are, to be able to live the Christian life and to pass on the Christian tradition to those that follow.

Traditioning comes by example and by teaching. We learn what it means to be Christian by imitating those with whom we share the community, and we learn by being taught the stories and the practices of the Christian Way. That means of course that the community surrounding those who are being "traditioned," themselves know the language, the stories and the practices so how well this happens will depend a great deal on the life within the congregation itself. Of course, it also depends upon how well the intentional teaching experiences are carried out, but if the community is not living as the person is being taught there is a disconnect in the nurture process.

So what does it mean to tradition someone? We can start with teaching the stories, the biblical narrative that provides the foundation for how we understand God and what it means to live in God's way. There are many effective methods for teaching the biblical stories and they need to be used in our group experiences and even in preaching. The point here is that our people need to know the key stories to catch the spirit of the Faith and the way to live exhibited there. This is especially true of the stories of Jesus and the prophets.

Of course, there are some ways of living in the Bible stories that we don't want to communicate, but that is a part of the challenge of teaching the Bible and we must learn how to choose what we teach and how to deal with the difficult stories.

One of my key issues is that what we teach from the Bible should be that which contributes positively to the person's relationship with God as well as how we should live. We have to be careful to not teach something that will turn someone away from God; unfortunately that is often easy if we are not discriminating about the way we teach from the Bible.

Then there is our needing to teach about what we believe, our theology. Again what we teach needs to help persons to understand the nature of God—of God's unconditional love—and the dynamic of our relationship with God—how it works, what it takes to be in relationship with God. The day is past when we can teach what we believe only for the purpose of someone knowing what we believe. What we believe needs to work in our lives.

Our theology then dovetails with our teaching of the spiritual disciplines as central practices of the Christian life. For too long we have left out the disciplines as functioning parts of our Christian practice and therefore have left out any help in how we relate to God. But you have heard a lot already about the centrality of the spiritual disciplines if you have read the previous sections.

Our traditioning also includes helping persons to know what it means to contribute to the ongoing life of the congregation through our money, our leadership, our participation in worship and study and how we show hospitality to those who come. All of these have to be a part, and a very intentional part, of nurturing effective servants of Christ.

Focus 3: Cultivating a Prophetic Stance— Being In But Not Of the World

This focus is one we may or may not have thought much about as a part of nurture but it is very important. It grows out of the need for us to be able to see clearly the ways in which we depend upon the culture around us for our meaning rather than upon God. It has to do with seeing the ways in which Christianity is truly countercultural if we are to follow Jesus. This is not making people hypercritical of what is happening in the world, but helping them to be wise as well as understanding of what is happening. It is about helping them to be able to take the stance of the prophets and of Jesus and see our culture for what it is when it is unloving, unjust and violent. It is as much about persons' inner ability to examine their dependence on the world as it is about what they are willing to do about the problems they find in our world.

Cultivating a prophetic stance involves teaching them the difference in the ways of the world and the ways of Jesus, helping them in their prayer to grow in their dependence upon God rather than the world and then, on the foundation of that knowledge and inner orientation, nurturing a prophetic sensibility.

It is probably obvious what it means to teach our people the difference in the ways of the world and the ways of Jesus. This should be a part of what we do in Traditioning as we talked above. How much we intentionally work on that is the question. Are we willing to truly tackle the kinds of things happening in our culture that are harmful to people's lives and against the spirit of Jesus and to help our people see how we are complicit in those ways? It is crucial to make it very obvious what being a Christian means we would be doing in our living every day, and how critical it is to stand up to the harmful directions of our culture. This will not be easy but if we are to have true servants of God's justice and peace, then our people will need to truly take up the ways of Jesus.

What will make it possible for people to resist the ways of the world is their growth in their dependence upon God for their meaning and not the world. It will be fundamental in the spiritual guidance we provide to help persons to learn how to examine the ways they look to the world for affirmation rather than to God. As they allow God to love them they will be more and more able to say no to what the world offers even in the midst of being very much a part of the world and loving the people in it. But it is an essential part of prayer to become aware of what we are doing and to allow God to free us from those tendencies. A prophetic sensibility is founded on both our learning the difference between the Christian way and the world's way and our inner, spiritual reorientation. But the functional sensibility also is nurtured in a community that has that sensibility and where that sensibility is made obvious in worship and whatever else happens. Our sensibility is strengthened by sharing in groups about how we feel about our culture and the problems we have in dealing with the challenges, so such sharing should be a regular part of the intentional nurture groups.

Focus 4: Servanthood—Being Servants of God's Justice and Peace

Servanthood is the ultimate goal of our nurture efforts. All else aims towards that result in the lives of our people. This focus has to do with the special content relating to servanthood specifically.

What we do in traditioning should include this, but to be specific, we must include the teachings of Jesus as to what it means to be loving, the prophets' concern with the importance of taking care of those in need and the Church's stance on social issues. We should be sure to point to the conditions in our world that need correcting and the need for systemic change, not simply charity, as important as that may be in specific situations.

Of course the fundamental content for servanthood will be the person's involvement in acts of servanthood, either individually or in a group. Servanthood experiences of all kinds, at all levels of difficulty should be offered over the course of a year. These experiences are best done when they are connected with teaching about the need and the proper preparation and training for the task.

A critical component of any servanthood nurture is that of reflection: reflection on the people and the need being served and on the presence of God in those people and in us. What is it that God is truly calling us to do in any specific situation so that we serve God's love and not our own need.

Servanthood experiences can be effective for nurture only if they are accompanied by the foundational teachings and the related information and spiritual reflection. We will look at this again in the commentary on the servanthood arena.

Arenas of Nurture

In Christian Nurture the concept of Arenas is an attempt to be more functionally specific about the ways in which nurture can effectively take place in a congregation. The approach proposes four arenas to focus our attention on intentional nurture: Congregational Environment, Nurture in the Home, Intentional Nurture in Groups, and Servanthood Nurture and Immersions. We believe these four to be key in helping us to provide an overall effort of effective nurture. The concept of the arenas and the commentary below are intended as guides for your designing and planning and are not meant to tie you to any forms or structures that might be implied in the presentation. You are responsible to use this information to design what is most meaningful for your congregation—being aware, however, of our suggestions as to what will make your efforts the most effective.

Arena 1: Congregational Environment
Congregational Environment is about what the name implies: creating within the congregation an environment that is more conducive

to effective nurture for all concerned. Everything that happens in the congregation nurtures or hinders faith in our people. That is something that is a given but something we don't always think about. Creating a positive nurturing environment means paying attention to all that is happening to see that it is the most faith nurturing experience possible. That takes attention and planning in all that is done. Some of the issues below will also be dealt with in other arenas, but this arena's concern is specifically what happens beyond the planning for those arenas.

It is suggested that this arena become a specific category (or structure if you desire) as you design your nurture ministry. It could become the work of a particular team of lay persons and certainly with staff participation.

What is included in a nurturing environment in the congregation?

- **People who are loving and caring**
- I assume that is an obvious element given the importance of our mirroring God's unconditional love to all we meet. What more will help the person to know they are loved by God, which is our key task, than to be loved by those who represent God's beloved people.
- **Experiences that relate persons to God and to each other**
- The most important thing we can do is to provide ways that persons truly encounter God from within and through each other. How can we help persons to sense the presence of God in worship, in group sessions and how can we create a deeper community among our people.
- **Traditioning experiences**
- It is a fundamental task for us to provide various ways in which our people come to know the stories and ways of the Christian faith and to come to cherish them. This needs to happen not just in the group experiences of Sunday School or other places, but in dramatic ways for instance in worship and at special events.

- **Experiences of Call**
- A part of nurture is also to confront each other with the demands of the Gospel—as long as we have first assured each other of God's unconditional love. This means to help persons to see the world, our culture, from God's perspective and be able to detach from it. It also means to call persons to service in ways they are most capable of responding.

Church Seasons and Congregational Environment

One of the best ways we can provide a nurturing, and especially a traditioning, environment is through the use of the Church Seasons as the guide to planning events within worship and beyond. The Seasons provide us not only with scriptural content but also with theological and life issue themes that can be expressed in various ways in cycles over the years so that there is repetition but also a balance of content.

Using these themes in worship or special events makes possible the use of drama and the arts that are aimed at communicating the content of the Gospel. This makes nurture more than simply listening to words in a sermon or presentation so that it can appeal to all the senses.

Some possible themes for each season can be found in the Appendix. You can also experiment with developing your own themes based upon the scriptural content of the lectionary and your own concerns for aspects of the Gospel message. We should never forget using current events as content to which we relate the themes of the Gospel.

Worship as Nurture

Worship is an especially critical time for nurture, especially when it is the place where we reach the majority of our people on a regular basis. The challenge of worship is to provide a time when folks can truly encounter God seeking to meet us in the flow of the service and the words of the music, scripture and sermon. It seems that worship must become a time when people are helped to move in their spirits from where they are to where God wants them to be in relationship to the particular focus of worship for that time. To see worship as nurture is to challenge us to explore how we can facilitate God's work with our people as they come to worship together.

To think for a moment of the classical movements of recognition of God (praise), recognition of who we are (confession), the hearing of the word of grace and of call (scripture and sermon) and our dedication to service: What will it take in the content of each of these to help persons to move spiritually from where they are to where God calls them to be? Worship also involves some teaching and guiding in the ways of our relating to God as well as to one another. How we use the scriptures is critical for effective nurture as well as the content and movement of the music and liturgy.?

Congregational Gatherings

When we gather as a congregation for special occasions, here again are times when effective nurture can take place. These can be times when relationships are built, community issues are explored and community bonds are developed around common directions. These can be times when drama and the arts can also come into play to expand the sense of who we are as a community of the beloved. These may be times when occasions of servanthood are celebrated and persons recognized and called so that all can catch the spirit of what it means to be servants.

Nurture in Administrative Settings

Several years ago now there was a spate of books and trainings on spiritual growth in administrative meetings. The focus was on how we can better bring what God is really calling us to do into our endless committee meetings so they become enriching times of Christian growth. That is still an important arena in which to seek to do nurture and there are still resources available to help us to do that in addition to the idea that we can probably do a good job on our own if our own spirituality is at the right place for it.

Arena 2: Nurture in the Home

We all know that what happens in the home is a more powerful instrument of Christian nurture than what happens in the congregation simply because the person spends a great deal more time in the home than in the congregation. It is more powerful, however, only if Christian nurture is actually taking place there. The time has gone when what the congregation does can depend upon it being a reinforcement and encouragement for what happens in the home, but maybe we can begin to return to some ways of restoring the strength of that element of nurture.

It seems that three activities can move us to strengthen the home for nurture.

First, we can see that parents themselves have a good foundation both in terms of their understanding of the Christian faith and an active personal spiritual journey.

Second, we can provide them with training in what Christian nurture in the home involves and give them support through groups and seminars, etc. They will need information and help in knowing how to guide their children's efforts at growing in their relationship with God.

Third, we can provide resources that the parents can use at home that reflect and reinforce what is happening in the nurture experiences in the congregation.

This will not be an easy task, but it is an accessible one. We can simply start at the point where parents are most cognizant of their need and build from there.

Arena 3: Intentional Nurture in Groups

The nurture of Christians through groups has always been the key domain of Christian education, the land of Sunday School and special courses, of Vacation Bible (or Church) School and weekday education. Implementing Christian Nurture may not change the settings, the groupings and times, but it will change what happens in those groups. Remember that we are leaving behind the focus on teaching the Bible and beliefs as an end in itself and the assumption that just learning about that body of knowledge will bring transformation. We are moving to provide that same learning so that it supports the inner, spiritual transformation and the way the person lives his/her life.

This arena can be very large with multiple planning teams working on various aspects or age level experiences, or it can be very simple in the small churches with one or two classes aimed at adult needs and whatever form of groups needed for children and youth. It is important to remember that our goal is not to simply provide classes but to nurture faith in our congregation. Therefore, the task is to do whatever that takes and to be creative in doing so. Focus on our objectives and let form follow function to be most effective.

The approach followed here is one where there is some concern for an overall design for what happens in the congregation while expecting design also in the various program areas of the congregation. The designing of what happens in this arena of group experiences will need to be done in concert with the overall design of the congregational environment (worship, special emphases, etc.) and of servanthood experiences and vice versa. This will call for cooperation between whatever groups do the planning for these arenas. The age level groupings will, of course, need to plan the specific experiences for that area of ministry and relate them to the overall design wherever possible. What happens here will also be the source for what happens in the resourcing of what parents can do in the home because we would hope that there would be a mutual reinforcing between these two arenas.

It is too easy to slight the effort necessary for the planning and then training of leaders in this arena of nurture, so special attention to those two elements is critical. What happens in these groups will deeply affect people in their Christian growth and so we must take them very seriously. People are searching in their lives for something to give them a sense of meaning even though they may not be aware of that search. It is our task to provide them with the opportunity to realize where they are in their spiritual journey and the resources in terms of concepts and relationships that help them to let God open them up and transform them.

Groups, especially the smaller more intimate opportunities for sharing, are of tremendous importance, but they must be well led by folks with the gifts to guide others on their journey. That is a tremendous challenge for us as we move toward a more effective nurture ministry. The small group may not be a study oriented group, but may focus on group spiritual direction or groups like Parker Palmer's circles of trust that help in a person's self awareness.

The content of Part Three is a series of chapters on the various aspects of designing and implementing nurture experiences. These are general guides that can apply to any of the areas of ministry but are specifically written with the arena of group experiences in mind.

Arena 4: Servanthood Nurture and Immersions

We assume that there is a lot of teaching about servanthood and what it means to be loving taking place in the intentional group experiences, but there is more to nurturing servanthood than that. First, it will be very important to help persons to become aware of their particular gifts and talents and of just what it is in the world that draws them to do something about. Those two things together define one's potential calling by God. Second, it is so very helpful to recognize and bless in a community gathering what a person is called to do and ways they have already served. Third, it is fundamental that persons are involved in hands-on service in a guided experience within the congregation's servanthood efforts—what we might call servanthood "immersions."

A congregation needs to set aside special opportunities for persons to get in touch with their gifts and talents through one of the various inventories available as well as through group sharing. People seem reticent to admit that they can do anything well so they need encouragement and the support of a caring group. Such self-awareness could be a part of the ongoing group nurture experiences or offered as special events with a major effort to get a high percentage of the people involved.

When persons are recognized for what they are doing or planning to do, it is deeply affirming to them and motivating to the congregation. Such times can be a very important part of a person's spiritual growth not to mention the ways it can energize the whole congregation. Such times can happen as a regular part of corporate worship when persons who are embarking on an individual or group servanthood effort are "commissioned" or "sent out" by the congregation. It may be a part of a special emphasis when folks can share their personal callings with the congregation. We too often forget the folks who are already, on their own, performing works of service to others so it will be important to find them and affirm their efforts.

Hopefully the congregation is providing opportunities for individuals to go as groups on "mission trips" or work projects. It may be that the congregation needs to plan such experiences as an intentional part of the nurture effort and not wait for the service opportunity to present itself. However the experience comes about, a critical part of that experience will be the preparation for the effort ahead of time, reflection on what is happening during the experience and a time of debriefing and reflection following it. Effective nurture through servanthood only happens when the times of preparation and reflection are present. Preparation sessions are times when the group is helped to understand who they are serving and what is really needed. They will examine their own inner reasons for being a part of the group and how the effort is an expression of God's compassion for those in need. During the event the group has a chance to share their personal experiences, how God has become more or less real to them through the experience, and how their contact with the persons they serve has affected them. After the event, participants are invited, for example, to evaluate the experience in terms of how helpful it truly was for those in need, what it meant to them spiritually and what it means for their future servanthood efforts.

Actual hands-on service in a guided experience is essential for truly effective nurture of persons for transforming the world. How that happens for each individual will be very different which is why we need to help them sort out what they are called to do at anyone point in their lives. If our people are not prepared for the experience, helped to reflect on what is happening to them and those they serve and then recognized for it, the effectiveness of the nurture potential is severely lessened or negated. To do this right takes some extra effort but it is the only way.

CHAPTER 8

ISSUES OF EFFECTIVENESS

There are certain issues about the content of our nurture experiences that present themselves as major items of concern as we implement a nurture ministry. Some you will find more compelling than others in your situation, but all are ones that need our careful attention if we are to be truly effective. There are some issues related to how we choose our content that are important to discuss. I am not trying to be prescriptive here but rather calling attention to what I consider to be important concerns as we decide what to offer in our ministry. Remember that the crying needs of our world are so loud these days that what we offer in our nurture must make a difference to those who are crying. Our choice of content also has to do with the effectiveness of our nurture. Remember what I said: effectiveness involves a focus on God and on being loving. The ideas that follow are of necessity partial dealings with these issues, so I hope that you will explore them further for yourself.

Scheduling of Content

In observing what happens in a local church nurture ministry, it is unfortunate that we find a program we think is great and we offer it once and never again. We may need to think about repeating those programs that are basic and most helpful. Repetition can be very helpful in the whole scope of nurture. We need to repeat certain things every month and year--about the Lord's Supper, about prayer, about things that we need to have set within our hearts. Not everyone can come to one event at a certain time, so if we want others to have that experience we need to repeat it. This is especially the case when we offer some basic course in our nurture curriculum.

It is also important to see that we do not leave out aspects of the Gospel message that need to be heard and just offer things we like to talk about. We tend to talk more about the more comfortable aspects of the message and leave out the harder calls to servanthood. More likely, without guidance we will keep hitting people over the head to do better and never talk about how God is always loving us.

We need a balance of content over our whole schedule of offerings and in our ongoing curriculum. This is the reason that I am a proponent of the use of the seasons of the Church year to shape the content of what we do. That is why the seasons exist. If we follow them and explore the possible themes within each season, we will be less likely to leave out something we need to talk about.

Is It Relevant to Our Objective?

Is what we decide to deal with in any of our nurture experiences relevant to the outcome we desire, and what God desires for our people? If you have worked out a meaningful, guiding objective, will you follow its guidance, or will you simply plan what seems to be popular or available at the moment? I believe that everything we decide to offer must be looked at under the light of our objective, otherwise we cease to be effective. If the objective seems to get in the way, then we need to look at how our objective is structured. The point here is to plan and implement that which will move us toward where we need and want to be--to seek intentionally to be effective in our nurture.

Our Approach to Scripture

To take seriously what I have said in the previous paragraphs means that we have to look at how we read the Bible. The Bible comes to us over centuries of being copied and recopied, through translation from one language to another more than once. It is prose and poetry and laws and letters--all written from a particular perspective with a particular purpose for the issues of the day and time in which it was written. It is best read as largely metaphor or story and with some level of acquaintance with its context. Certainly we also need to just sit down with it and read it as it speaks to us where we are.

How do we go about helping others through its web of content? I read a story recently that recounted an experience in which the pastor of a local church had not really leveled with his people about the modern scholarship related to the Bible for fear of what they would think and say. When his people did hear about that scholarship they accused the pastor of previously lying to them and ask that he be dismissed from their church. [20] We don't trust our people enough in what we teach them about our sacred scripture.

Whether we read the Bible literally or metaphorically, the real issue is what does any particular passage mean for our lives. Whatever the topic, the only important thing is that we gain some kind of "word from the Lord" about how much God loves us and what we ought to do today and tomorrow in our living. Further, if we call ourselves Christian that means we read it through the eyes of Jesus and the Spirit and ask the question again. I was always taught that any part of the Bible stands under the judgment of Christ, of Jesus and of the Holy Spirit. We cannot simply say it means this or that because of our particular leanings or cultural predispositions or our personal opinions.

It is our task to help our people to see and be able to read the Bible in a way that is helpful to them and not one that scares them off from what it has to offer. We must help them to approach it with some acquaintance with up-to-date biblical scholarship but also through the loving eyes of Jesus and the unconditional love of God. We must help them to read it with a questioning, searching eye and heart and read it within their prayer, letting its words soak into them and flow over them so that the Spirit can speak through the words.

The Bible is a difficult, complicated book in many ways, but it is our sacred scripture and we have to take it seriously. How we approach it, however, is of greatest importance. The real test of what we teach from the scripture, as Jesus points out, is the fruit that it bears in our actions. From Jesus' example, that fruit is loving and inclusive above all else.

Being Developmentally Appropriate

One of the foundational issues in education is whether what is done is developmentally appropriate--i.e., does it take seriously the developmental stage of persons both whether they can understand it cognitively and whether it is relevant to their lives. What is appropriate has to do with the methods used as well as the content.

This is very important in the case of how we use the Bible and it is especially the case with young children. The Bible is an adult book and not all the passages are usable with young children and in some cases with early elementary children. This has to do with the cognitive development of the person as well as the ability to find meaning in the content itself. It would be so helpful if we would follow the rule that says we do not teach people something about the Bible that they will have to unlearn later. This does not mean that children do not need to be acquainted with the scriptures; it only means that we carefully choose which passages we use with them and are careful to help them to understand the existential meaning of the passages and not see them as literal unless they are.

Being developmentally appropriate is so important for children because they are moving so fast through the cognitive as well as social and physical stages of development, but it is also critical at any age. Methodologically, it is better, for instance, to use centers in children's experience and give them choices. How long they can be still depends on their age. For youth, more active and interactive experiences are better. For adults and youth, methods are tied more to effectiveness in learning than to developmental stage, of course, where the concern is more the relevance of the content. Related to content, youth have only technically reached abstract thinking ability by age 12 years, so the content for early adolescent years must be looked at carefully in the sense of understanding why they react as they do to what is being shared. In older adolescence we need to be more open to their intellectual quests and the need for questioning, providing them with the challenges of what this Faith is really all about. Then for adults there is the need to be aware of the developmental stage issues they face, such as parenting, job issues, stresses of responsibility. For the older years we can be so helpful in providing perspectives on the years of later life and a focus on the deeper spiritual issues those years call forth. It is best when adults can choose what they want to experience, so we need to be sensitive to how we go about planning for adult needs and try to include them in the decision making process when possible.

About Theological Content

Years ago I was introduced to a profoundly helpful statement that says: "Theology without spirituality is dead; spirituality without theology is dangerous." What we teach theologically is of great importance. First, what we say about God will affect how people relate to God and whether they allow God to love them, or even believe that God is a loving God. At the same time, it is crucial that we understand that Christianity is a way of life, a path to new life, not simply a set of beliefs to which we subscribe. It is not what we believe that saves us, but our relationship with God. To say it again, what we come to think about God affects our relationship with God.

Theology is one of the key arenas in which we interact with the person's Intellect, that faculty that involves what we think, how we reason about an issue. What is so important in this arena is that persons are free to recognize what they do think about an issue and free to think differently from the leader and others if that is where they are. People need to be free to question whatever theological ideas they come across. We cannot coerce people into thinking a certain way; we can only offer them ideas, ways of thinking about an issue and allow them to come to what they think. Our experiences in life give us perceptions and perspectives that will enter into how we see something new that is presented to us. How we feel about ourselves at a particular time will affect how we receive what is being offered, whether we feel safe enough to entertain a new idea or not. That is why the leader of an experience in thinking about the theology of our Faith must be someone who is willing to provide an emotionally and intellectually safe environment if meaningful nurture is to take place.

When we go about teaching theology or about what we believe as Christians, it is crucial that we teach it in a way that nurtures persons' relationship with God, that informs their prayer as well as their living. We cannot continue to teach theology for its own sake. How does what we believe function in our lives as well as how can I understand it in today's terms? What does it mean to say, "Jesus died for my sins," in what I can do differently in my life. Just to say that is what we believe does not get us down the road to being a servant people. This is saying the same thing I said about the Bible. We have to teach the Bible not for the sake of teaching the Bible, but for the sake of the person's life with God.

A sound, faithful, theology can keep us from going off the deep end with how we see life. There are many, many teachers of spiritual practices in our world today and there are so many people seeking life through some kind of path. Some of those paths might be helpful to certain people, some may be very harmful, but how will they know. When we teach theology that is sound, whether it is more traditional or more progressive (to use those difficult terms), if it is done well, in the Spirit of Jesus, in God's love, it will help persons to be able to discern what is helpful in their world and what is not.

Our understanding of God has been called the central theological issue of our day. Whether God exists and what kind of god is God are the biggest ones. Our nurture issues must deal fully with the nature of God and take seriously the perspectives of scripture and help people try to resolve for themselves the seeming and real conflicts we find there about who God is and do it in a way that is true to Jesus' perspective, taking nothing out of context. I find the issues of God and suffering and the view of God as judgmental and violent are so problematic to so many people and are so relevant to issues in todays world. If, for instance, God is seen as a violent, punishing God then we are more likely to be violent and punishing ourselves. This is crucial stuff! How

God is seen is related to how we act. The realm of ethics and morals is fundamentally a theological issue. What does God say about war and about the many other deeply troubling issues of our day? I have been reminded in reading some Old Testament theology of the deep concern for distributive justice that is attributed to God. How well do we speak of the relationship between the justice of our actions toward the less fortunate and the quality of the life in our world community. It may be that we need to speak more about the consequences of our ways upon the condition of our world.

Our theology cannot be taught from an exclusivist perspective. To say that Christianity is the only way is harmful to our own witness to God's love in our world. If you don't happen to agree with me about this, that's OK for now--just think about it. Was Jesus exclusive in his relationships? Of course, this goes back to how we read the scriptures. May God help us in our reading and in our teaching.

If there is any arena where theological "reeducation" and meaningful formational experiences need to take place, it is with adults. Let's not short change our adults, but get them involved in some relevant, in-depth theological thinking for their sake and for the sake of the church.

Finally, and I am repeating myself, what we teach will be judged by its fruits in the lives of our people. I have no problem with anyone's theological perspective as long as its result is our being open, accepting, loving servants of others. Think about it that way as you decide what to teach.

Including the Spiritual Disciplines

In case you have not understood my concern by now, let me say again that the spiritual disciplines must be central to the content of our nurture experiences. If we are not enabling our people to enter and nurture a relationship with God, then we are not doing our job. We cannot assure it happening or make them do that, but we have to do everything possible to open the door, prepare them and encourage them to do so. A personal (direct) relationship with God is absolutely central to Christian nurture and the spiritual disciplines are central to nurturing our relationship with God.

We often don't remember that people do not necessarily know how to pray in a way that is helpful to them. Fortunately we are beginning to learn about the varieties of prayer forms, in many ways thanks to the eastern religions pushing us Christians to dig back into our own past. People need more than verbal prayers of intercession and petition. They also need to know what silence is about and how to pray in a receptive mode; to use centering prayer as well as praying with the scriptures; to use the labyrinth and other prayer forms. There is so much richness in the Christian traditions of prayer that we can help people to claim as their own and thereby help their relationship with God grow richer.

How many people really understand the meaning of the sacraments? We observe the Lord's Supper on some kind of regular basis, but how many can see it, for instance, as the wonderful metaphor it is of God feeding us with love and not simply remembering the sacrifice of Jesus. Baptism also has much more richness than we help folks to see; that it too is a proclamation of God's unconditional love and not an exclusionary initiation rite that divides us from others.

We could go on about the wonderful experiences that await persons who learn the depth and richness of the spiritual disciplines. We can also go on to not only teach the disciplines but provide for personal guides through one-on-one and group spiritual direction. Spiritual direction or guidance is simply helping people to let God help them. It is helping persons to talk about and better understand their relationship with God and gain some help in going further in their growth in that relationship. Spiritual direction is a growing ministry in the church today and more and more persons are being trained in the art. We do need to remember, however, that being a spiritual director or guide is a gift and no amount of training will make you one even through training is important. People who seek guidance should be helped to see that the relationship with a guide is a very personal one and that if one relationship does not feel helpful then they should go to another until they find one that is helpful. In many cases our friends can become our spiritual guides and that means that the more we can do to help persons to understand the nature of the spiritual life, our life with God, the more we can simply help each other.

A potential content for any or all group settings that has been put forth in various ways in recent years is the inclusion of some way of helping bring God's presence into the experience. Maybe this could only be through prayers at the beginning and end, but it might also be, for instance, a time of silence at the appropriate time to allow the Spirit to enter the conversation. It might be a time of looking at relevant scripture in the midst of an administrative meeting and inviting some spiritual discernment around the issues at hand. I am not recommending that we go back to the practice of a full "devotional" time at the beginning of a meeting, which became more of a waste of time in most cases. We are called to think creatively about how God can become a part of each experience. Of course, any such effort must be relevant to the other content of the experience or it will be irrelevant itself.

Nurturing Servants of God's Justice and Peace

Nurture experiences that deal with the social, ethical, moral, and justice dimensions of our Faith are the ones that begin to focus on the result of our nurture efforts. All else we do moves us toward this outcome in the lives of our people. If that does not happen then we have not been effective. However, given the understanding that we do not really control what happens, we can only make it more possible. Nurture efforts in this arena include, but certainly move beyond, information processing.

What we teach in the information sharing sessions about servanthood, of course, starts with Jesus' teachings, the Old Testament and later scripture witnesses and then with what the Church has taught over the centuries as the interpretation of those scriptures. Immediately we run into the problem--the "interpretation" of the scriptures. I will refer you to what I said above about how we have to look at the Bible through the eyes of Jesus and the Spirit of God. Even then we will come out differently and have to move to something more simple and basic--we are called to do what is loving to God and to each other. Here is where the nature of God we share becomes important. Is God a God who truly cares first about those in need, the homeless and the hungry, etc.; or is God a God who cares first about what we think is pure and obedient--the following of the letter of what seems to be the Law? Or is God both and we have to understand the difference and the balance God wants.

There must be sessions where we look hard at what is happening in our world in the light of the Gospel message, Jesus' teachings, the Ten Commandments, etc. The Gospel is a political and economic as well as spiritual message because it concerns where we place our loyalties and how we look at the problems of our society. We cannot help but talk about those kinds of issues and we can do so without "taking sides" for one candidate or another. It is also important to help persons to share about their own personal struggles with ethical and moral issues--again, that is why we have to provide an emotionally and intellectually safe environment along with confidentiality. At bottom these are spiritual issues in terms of our personal willingness to engage the social problems head on. Am I secure enough in God's love for me, in my being beloved, so that I have the courage to stand up to the "powers that be" for the sake of the Gospel?

This realm of nurture pushes us beyond simply sitting in a group and learning about the Ten Commandments and what they mean--though that is essential. Dealing with what is loving pushes us to be in touch with each other and with those whom God cares about who need us. It pushes us to experience being with those in need, seeking to understand them and then to do what we can do to help them move out of their situation to a better one. It is very clear and crucial for us to realize that there is a difference between simple charity and working for systemic justice. Charity is important but it cannot be a replacement for work we can do toward changing the systems that create injustice. Here is where we truly enter the realm of what it means to be a servant of the Kingdom of God. That is why these experiences require times of group sharing and prayer about what is happening within us as well as with those we are seeking to serve. We cannot do service projects without some time for group reflection.

Probably one of the most overlooked aspects of nurture in servanthood is to discover those who are being servants on their own, so to speak, outside the programs of the church and involve them in some kind of support and reflection group. There are so many of our people doing volunteer work, being servants in the home with those in need that we often don't see and know about. Let's find them and honor them and support them for their service to the Kingdom.

A Relationally Safe and Physically Supportive Environment

Where an experience takes place and the emotional environment are as much a part of the content of the experiences as what is said and shared. Environment communicates something to the person. The physical environment says that the person is either cared for or ignored in terms of needs--temperature, light, arrangement, etc., are all important. The conditions do not have to be new or special, but they do need to be warm and inviting. The relational or emotional environment is even more important. Is is safe to say what I feel? Will people keep confidences? Am I accepted as part of the group? These are some of the questions people ask within themselves when they come to a group. The provision for such concerns is just as important as anything else we plan for.

Using Information Technology to the Greatest Advantage

There are few churches that do not now have their own web sites, but whether they are used to the greatest advantage for nurture is another matter. As it was when videotape came into use in the church, such media is not the answer in all cases and there is much being written about its pros and cons. There are valuable uses in online courses for youth and adults and in the social media, maybe even for children and certainly for leadership training. We must still provide for and encourage face to face groups to deeply nurture our relationships, however much we make use of the technology. Media will be valuable in reaching people and in providing for information communication when folks can't come to a group session.

Reflection

Can you think of other and possibly even more compelling issues than these? Take note of them for the sake of your ministry.

THE END OF PART 2
A SPECIAL NOTE

There are about three times as many pages in discussing the foundations of nurture as there are pages about the task itself. That is because the task itself is simple in outline and though challenging to implement, only each congregation can fulfill all that the task involves. I cannot detail what needs to happen in each congregation; each congregation has to design what will be helpful in its particular situation using the objective and the guide of what the task involves. I am sure that most congregations, if not all, will need help in designing an effective nurture ministry in that we have not done it this way before. That help can be available but the congregations have to ask for it and see that they get it—remember, we have to take responsibility for our nurture ministry!

I suppose the question in the present climate in the Church in which Christian education has taken a back seat, is whether the congregations and the church at large are really concerned, beyond paying lip service, to really do something about the situation and begin to see that nurture is returned to its place of essential importance. I just heard a presentation by Kenda Creasy Dean about the situation in which we find our youth now in America who are not that concerned about the church or about religion. Their stance is really a reflection of where we as adults are in our concern for the Church and our lack of emphasis on the importance of religion, of a relationship with God in Christ. The future is here and we are called to be faithful and we are called to do all we can to see that our people, our children, youth and adults, find that which God has for them in their lives here and now so they can become loving servants of God's justice and peace.

What I have shared is a vision of what needs to be done. It is certainly not the last word and not even the first word. It is only a vision among many. It is up to all of us to work out what the future will be. Next in Part 3 are some suggestions for designing and implementing a nurture ministry.

PART THREE

IMPLEMENTING A NURTURE MINISTRY

In spite of what has been said that this is not a "how to" book or program, I am counting on the local church leadership to be able to do the designing and management of the future nurture ministry. So it seems important to also provide some practical ideas to be as helpful as possible.

I believe, rightly or wrongly, that we have forgotten some of the things that made our earlier efforts at Christian education more helpful and effective. I believe that people at whatever age and in whatever culture we find them are all seeking the same things. There are concepts and skills that we have learned about how people learn and change and how best to help them to change that will not be different whether they see themselves to be only spiritual or religious or both, or have been in the church all their lives or are just finding it. We have found that certain things help persons to grow better than others so we need to use those practices. Certainly we must be aware of the contemporary styles and forms persons now use to communicate and learn, but whether they are viewing a video on YouTube or participating in a traditional Sunday School class the same best practices apply. There are certainly some things from the past that need to be discarded, but there is much that needs to be retained and reinstated for use. What follows is an attempt to share those concepts and processes.

It is important to make sure that readers hear my concern that they see these ideas not as a set format for the only way, but as guides and principles that can be applied in any size congregation. No one and no written material can implement the ministry—only you, using your ideas and the help you find, can make it the most effective possible ministry.

Nurture is and can be a part of all that we do and also be found in specific, intentional, well-balanced, relevant experiences for our people so that they will continue to grow in their acceptance of God's love for them and their commitment to servanthood in the world. What follows is a section on designing a nurture ministry, a chapter on settings, on methodology and on leadership. I truly hope you will find some helpful ideas among these pages that will make the development of our nurture ministry more effective and enjoyable.

Chapter 9

Designing a Nurture Ministry

Designing is something we do all the time to some degree, but not always as it is needed. Designing is the factor that moves us from what we intend to what happens to fulfill the intention. Whether we are actually effective is determined by many other factors, but if the design is not on target we have less chance to reach that effectiveness.

The popular phrase today, in the United Methodist Church at least, when you talk about planning, is "discipleship systems." The intent is a good one as I understand it and is the same as my own intent: to help the local church to develop intentional processes and experiences that will grow up disciples or, in my phrasing, servants of the Kingdom. You may have already attended or plan to attend some form of training in such system design and that is good. What you will find here hopefully will add positively to what you are gaining in those experiences.

As I have mentioned elsewhere, what we are designing is not a program, not a Sunday School, but a way of nurturing faith in persons. The setting, the content, the leadership are all resources planned so that they contribute to the nurturing. That means that what happens may at times step beyond some of our traditional settings, but it can just as well mean that we are using the traditional settings in different ways, in better, more effective ways. There is always the need for innovation, but not for the sake of innovation. The important issues are the persons and the relationships coming together in the presence of God who is always there, and that can happen anywhere when we bring love to the experience. Of course, there are certain experiences that will better communicate to some persons than others and that needs to be considered in the designing. Do not think that you cannot do effective, loving nurture if you don't have certain equipment, technology, space or whatever; just plan with whatever you have and bring God's love and your love to it. So as you read what I have shared below about designing just remember to see these ideas as ones to provide you with perspective and to use or not use in whatever situation you find yourself.

Factors in Design

There are three factors or sources of input in designing: 1) the life situation and needs of the people you serve, 2) the content of the Gospel, and 3) the aspects of faith that we talked about earlier. Leave out either one of these and you risk being ineffective or irrelevant or both.

The life situation of the people comes also from at least two directions: 1) the developmental needs, and 2) the present existential factors in their living. We can do a lot to plan for the developmental needs in a theoretical way. For instance, because we know something about the developmental stage characteristics of a 5 year old, we can know basically what to do in a group setting that will be helpful to that child and any 5 year old. This is also the case with any age group because there are some things that take place at each developmental stage that can be used in our design strategy. You begin with the theory and then move to the specific needs of the persons in the group.

Developmental needs also include an awareness of the movements of spiritual growth. There are adults as well as children who were never really taught the basics of prayer or how to read the scripture. Then there are those who have progressed on their journey who need an ever- deepening experience to guide them further in their relationship with God.

The existential factors will have to come from our knowledge of our people and what is happening in the world and the community at any particular time. These existential factors also contribute to the spiritual status of our people. To use present day issues and deal with them in the light of the Gospel is very important. It brings so much relevance to what we are doing which means that people will more readily be open to what we are offering.

The content of the Gospel is best approached, in my opinion, first of all, by using the Church year to structure the flow of experiences, not in any hard and fast manner, but as a guide for what happens over the course of a year. Each season of the year has certain themes that can be used in worship but also in planning the content of nurture experiences for that time of year. (See the Appendix for some possible themes for each season.) This better assures a balance in the content of the Gospel presented and keeps us from dealing only with our favorite subjects. I personally think it is helpful to go back to an older structure of the seasons in the UMC where we had the season of Kingdomtide from September 1 to Advent which gives us another more focused set of themes for that time of year.

It may be helpful to point out, and we will discuss this later also, that there is planning for the present needs of persons to which the Gospel can speak, a pastoral form of nurture, but there is also planning for intentional nurture that presents the full scope of the Gospel through out the life span of the individual. What I am sharing here will address both, but you will need to be aware of which is which and not short change either one. Our tendency is to offer those experiences that meet the moment's needs because they make it easier to get folks to come, but our folks may be missing some of the deeper aspects of the Faith that they need. The use of the church year in planning speaks to this need. Just be sure to provide other kinds of experiences that pull the people deeper than they think they can go.

Another way to approach the Gospel content interwoven with the Church Year is the developing of a "curriculum areas" form of structure. For instance, my congregation has just instituted a curriculum form that includes four areas: nurturing our relationship with God, servanthood in the world, exploring the scriptures and exploring our beliefs. In another congregation we had six areas that added two to the above four:

relationships and Church history. Under each of the major headings then there would be various topics that could be developed to touch on the needs of the persons involved. What areas you use are, of course, entirely up to your creativity. There is no one way to create such a list. The important thing is that by using such a listing you have a guide so that you will not leave out something that is important.

I am sure that you can see that if you create a matrix with the seasons and themes of the church year on one axis and the life situations and developmental needs of the people organized through the curriculum areas on the other, you will have a way to decide what you need to offer in any one year. You will want to consider the rotating of the themes in the seasons through the different years. For instance, in year one for Lent you may want to deal with personal prayer; in year two you focus on being reflective about the inner life, etc. Here is where you can hold to the general themes of Lent but also bring in a particular life issue that is present in your congregation at the moment. Also, if you are pursuing a major emphasis throughout the year, the particular way you approach that emphasis would be guided by the Gospel themes in each particular season.

Finally, as you are setting out the different content focused experiences, make sure that you are also providing a balance of types of experiences that nourish the different aspects of faith—the Spirit, the Intellect and the Will. It is too easy to simply think of informational or more "cognitive" types of experiences and forget that to reach the whole person we also need experiences that touch their spirits as well as involve them in actual practice of being loving and committing to servanthood. If you have caught the vision of integrating spiritual formation and education you will be doing this. Some of this balance will come as you design the details of each experience, but it will be helpful to look at it from the overall perspective. For instance, are we making sure that there are meaningful servant experiences and times where persons are helped to consider their inner spiritual concerns.

Why go through all of this? It may seem so complicated! You go through it if you want to be effective over the long haul in your ministry. It is important to touch all aspects of the Gospel and our life situations and to repeat those things that we want persons to carry with them into their daily lives. Once you begin to practice "going through all of this," you will do it without thinking about it. For instance, once you come up with a content area design and a matrix that you can refer to it gets easier. We are not in this task to just lazy through it. It takes effort and if we don't make the effort we cannot expect the results we would like to have. Remember, the results we want are not just more people and people having fun; we want people who will be God's servants of justice and peace.

The Design Process

When we have talked about nurture in the past we usually have meant Christian education, which in turn suggests a certain group of people and processes that do not necessarily work together with other agencies. I ask you to lay aside any previous conceptions about such structures and think differently for a moment. There are at least three major levels of design to be considered. First is the overall, congregational level of design and the second is the design of the particular areas of ministry—age levels, worship, social concerns, etc.—and third, the design of the individual nurture experiences.

A word about different settings for design: What I am sharing must be seen as theoretical in that we need to take the basic ideas and work them around to fit where we are. Designing nurture will look very different in the very small church than it does in the larger churches with staff, so don't take these ideas without adaptation to where you are. The ideas are presented imaging a church with at least some "program planning" groups, but in a small situation that may mean three or four people. (See the section below on the small church.)

Overall Congregational Direction

Since everything the congregation does contributes to Christian nurture, there should be some way that all of the "ministry areas" could come together to do the overall designing of the outlines of nurture experiences. This may take some refocusing of how we approach designing program. Usually, each of the ministry areas brings their proposals for the future to a meeting to "report" on what they want to do and the process then is simply one of meshing calendars.

I propose that we step back a notch and begin to ask the question what is it that as a congregation we need to focus on in the next six months or a year? Start at least a good six months or more ahead of time of course. You start with the season's themes in light of what you have done in the past and ask the questions of what aspect of the Gospel will help our congregation grow in this day and time and what is happening in the world and in our people's lives to which we need to speak. We do this first as a united group, without reference to our own areas. Here is where we try to use the "matrix" of themes and needs suggested above.

At some point, bring up the guidelines of the Arenas of Nurture from Chapter Seven and see if you have included efforts in all of these arenas. This will help insure that your nurture efforts will be more effective in the lives of your people.

After we have put forth a general direction, in the second level of design each group develops their suggestions that support or complement that direction. Certainly there may be programs that are needed that don't fit neatly into the overall theme and ones that are needed whatever the theme is, but it will be important to be intentional about what we do so that there is a greater impact in our ministry. All of the planning is then brought together for final coordination and implementation. Remember that a group that doesn't usually plan "educational" experiences may still plan a nurture experience if it is handled as such. This is especially true for social concerns or mission group experiences. Even the stewardship group often plans some kind of nurture (educational) segment to their efforts. I believe it is important to see more of the nurture efforts extended to relate to the usually "non-nurture" aspects of our ministry.

Many churches still have some kind of "program" council or ministry council that oversees the programing of the congregation's activities. Too often that group is too caught up in the minutiae to do creative work, but just maybe a new focus on nurture could ignite a creative surge. It may not be really helpful to have some additional group do the initial thinking because that means the program deciding group will not really own what they come up with. If we can get our leaders thinking creatively about what needs to be done and not simply responding to ad hoc thinking we may find some new energy and effective results. The creativity will come when we think about the Gospel themes and the needs of our people first without reference to details. Note that this is changing the order of what usually happens and puts the overall thinking first followed by the designing by the different program areas. Such a process is also the way to begin to include some time of prayerful discernment about ministry directions. Spend some time, for instance, helping the group understand the themes in the church seasons, or do some brief, theme-related bible study to help focus the group on being creative and not getting caught in the details. I do recommend that in these planning times that you set aside any consideration of details and asking for reports from groups. That can come later.

Ministry Level Design

The second level of design is that of the ministry grouping which we noted above. Here we take the overall directions and concerns raised in the general planning and develop the specific programs that would provide the needed nurture. In a particular age group you might be looking at programs in all of the Ministry Arenas to keep the balance. Then you would want to plan for content of those programs that involved the four Focuses of Content. It may be that a particular program would carry only one of the focuses or a program might contain more than one of the focuses. For instance you might plan a class on prayer for youth or the Advent Festival might include experiences that expressed three of the focuses in the various experiences offered.

The point is that as you plan experiences to meet the Gospel concerns and the life situations of the people you use the Focuses of Content as a guide to be sure that you are including a balance of content that will yield greater long-range nurture effectiveness.

Let's look now at the age level areas. Most churches still have some kind of age level committees that have usually focused on Sunday school and other age related activities. They would participate in the direction-setting designing and then plan creatively what needs to happen within their particular age group. These age level groups would, therefore, need to see their work in a larger perspective and begin to take responsibility for some overall "curriculum" design that would work together with everything else the church is doing as well as contribute to the overall direction along with meeting the particular developmental needs of the age group. What happens on Sunday in worship should have some mutual relationship to what happens in Sunday school for children, for instance, especially on some basis, though not every week. It will not be helpful to have worship always dictate the content of children's SS classes, but the seasonal themes could be worked into both worship and the SS class content so that there is some form of connection that is helpful. Here is where the planners would need to consider the design for intentional formation in the Faith for the age group as well as the relationship with the congregational directions.

The design for Sunday morning experiences for children and youth will certainly involve some form of resource that provides a long-range curriculum of content that has a cycle of themes over 2 to 3 years. Most congregations will not be able to design their own, so they will purchase such a resource, hopefully after careful consideration. Integrating the overall congregational design with those resources means that the age level planning group does not accept a purchased curriculum resource as is. Instead, what happens every week is looked at in light of the overall content themes of the life and the weekly sessions designed with developmentally appropriate activities that create an "environment" in which the children see connections and learn and grow.

There will always be content and experiences that should be provided for children and youth (hopefully provided by the resources chosen for use) that cannot be taken care of simply by following a congregational theme direction. That is also one of the problems in using a lectionary-based resource. Therefore the age level design team must see that the basic content needed is present while at the same time integrating the overall congregational themes as described above. I cannot emphasize strongly enough that age level design teams must custom redesign whatever resource they use as they go through the year.

It is important to consider other groupings than age levels such as parents, intergenerational experiences, special needs such as young marrieds, divorced persons, marriage preparation, etc. If we are to more effectively improve the nurture of our children it will mean reaching them through their parents at home. The need is certainly upon us to do more for older adults to aid them in their continued spiritual growth. Their numbers in our churches is steadily increasing and present a crucial arena for ministry as it has always been. This is certainly a part of a nurture ministry that is life long.

There are of course other ministry areas, especially social concerns and worship, which will take the overall design that is offered and see what it means for their area of concern. Worship planners will need to be sensitive to the nurture function they perform as they plan and design the services so that their worship experiences are not simply performances but times when people are helped to move spiritually within themselves and with each other. This is not at all to take away from what worship is about, but to make it even more effective. The area of social concerns or "church and society" is a key arena for nurture and should see itself in that light. The experiences they plan should be helped to interface with the age level groups as well as worship, and they should make use of all of the group process skills and approaches to fulfill their task. This arena is key to our people understanding more deeply the nature of servanthood for "transformation of the world." It is their task not simply to put forth service projects, but to do consciousness raising and "compassion nurture" as a part of their effort.

Designing Specific Nurture Experiences

Once the content is decided upon and we begin to plan a course and/ or the individual sessions, there are other aspects to be determined—the setting, providing a balance among the aspects of faith, the inclusion of the key experiences and methods, and the determination of the leadership needed.

Planning the settings to be used, if not already in place such as Sunday School, means simply deciding what kind of grouping and when and where it will be best to offer which experiences. (See Chapter 8 on Settings.) Some of those decisions will of course already be determined by the church season and other kinds of congregational or community scheduling. The choice of settings is especially important in making it more possible for persons to attend and to increase the effectiveness.

You will want to be sure that you have experiences within each of the sessions you design that provide a balance of the aspects of faith, which means that you will want to have not only informational or intellectual experiences but also ones where people's feelings and deeper concerns are dealt with and times when they are invited to actually practice behaviors and make commitments. Most of this balance will come as a result of using the key experiences (see Chapter 4 and the short listing below), but it will be helpful to at least be aware of how the experiences touch on the different aspects of faith.

Using the key experiences, you will look at the content and see where you can most effectively use each of the experiences. Some of them will be used regularly, others in special experiences. The point is to be sure not to leave out any of the experiences over the course of the time frame you are designing. That is the way we will be sure to touch the whole person. Remember that the key experiences are actually references to categories of methods, and so you will be determining the key experiences along with the methods that are best to use. For instance, in "sharing" you may want to use a buzz group method. (See the section on methods for more information.)

So much of the time, at this level of planning, we are using some kind of resource that has already done much of this for us. Even if we have such resources they must be redesigned to fit the nurture intention, the people involved, etc. There is never a piece of resource that should be used without being reworked. It is too easy, especially in the case of age level resources to just hand leaders the resource and tell them to "teach it," which means that we really don't know what will result from it and whether it will be effective nurture for our situation.

There are resources such as DVD presentations, other A/V material, books, resource persons, that can be meaningfully used within a designed session to do what we intend to do. I believe that this is especially true for adult nurture since such resources provide the kind of expertise and insight that may not be available from within your group. But, I repeat, these resources should be used as a part of the experience that is carefully planned around them for greater effectiveness. (Chapter 10 on methods talks in more detail about session planning.)

One of the very critical issues for us today is in the arena of adult formation. There are so many adults who have little or no involvement in growing in their faith and a large part of the problem is in what we are offering. So much of the published curriculum resources for adults are shallow and sermonic in their content. This is an arena where the local church truly needs to take responsibility for assessing the true needs and situations of its adults and provide experiences that are vital and help persons encounter God in their lives in a real way. I know this is not easy for some adult groups, but let's not leave the other adults out. Here is where the use of the many DVD-based courses that are available can be used to bring expertise to the experience that local folks may not have.

It may be that you believe your congregation does not have the expertise to pull off such planning. You may be surprised, however, at what you will be able to do if you will make the effort. First, look around in your congregation for those who have had training in the educational process, even curriculum design. If you still need help, go to the Conference Council office (in the UMC) and ask for persons who can come and help you to learn to do this. That is what it will take if we are to be more effective in our task! Finally, whatever our level of expertise, if we go about this with a desire to be truly effective and not just provide "any old" experience and be open to the Spirit working within us, we will be amazed at what will happen.

In this kind of approach there can be no hard and fast rules. What I have shared are ideas from my own experience and training. The key is to first of all meet the needs of the people we serve in the light of the

Gospel message and then be concerned to be as intentional and effective as possible in our nurture. All of our processes have to be subservient to those efforts. A way to check ourselves in our designing might be to ask the following questions that seek to help you get at some of the practices that are very important.

1. Developmentally appropriate practices: Are the methods and content of the experiences appropriate to the age group involved?
2. Is there a balance of content over the whole Gospel?
3. Life relevance: Are the topics and methods used to deal with them relevant and appropriate to the life situation of the person, child, youth or adult?
4. Have we included the key experiences that are relevant to the session?
5. Is there present an emotionally safe and caring environment?
6. Is the physical environment appropriate and inviting and comfortable?
7. Do the leaders exhibit loving care for the individuals in their group?
8. Does the design of the experience take seriously the present activity of God in the group?

Listing of Key Experiences (See Chapter 4 for descriptions.)
Awareness
Expression
Information Communication
Interaction/Interpretation
Practice/Action-Reflection
Sharing
Committing

Reflection

What questions do you have? What is missing here? Which of the suggestions do you want to try to use?

CHAPTER 10

SETTINGS FOR NURTURE

One of the aspects of designing is to determine what kind of "setting" is best for accomplishing what you intend. A "setting," for our purposes, is a combination of characteristics of an experience that includes kind of grouping, time and location. The Sunday School is a setting of a particular kind as is a work group experience. Settings become a part of your design as you plan for the group of persons involved, the kind of experience desired and the most convenient time frame.

There are many innovations taking place in the church today, but whatever the innovation it will probably be in one of the basic forms I mention below. They may take place outside the church walls, at the mall, the coffee shop, etc., but they still will be small group, large group, etc.

The Home

It seems appropriate to mention this setting first since it is the very basic setting where children, youth and adults receive a lot of spiritual nurture or a lack of it. The children who come to us have spent a lot more time in the home than they will ever spend in the nurture experiences of the church. If we cannot impact what is happening there we will not make as much headway as we need to. Of course, what happens in the home is guided by the adults, which means that they are the ones we need to focus on if we are to more fully nurture our children in the most positive way. So as important as our Sunday School and other activities for children and youth are we need to work hard at how we can make a difference in what happens in the home.

Among the efforts we need to make are the following:

Nurture the parents in their own spiritual growth. How can they nurture their children and youth if they are not there themselves?

Provide training for the parents in the stages of child/youth development, guiding their children in loving ways, forms of prayer appropriate to their children's ages, how children/youth grow spiritually and how they can nurture that growth.

Provide resources for parents to use with their children and even a resource for youth to take home or have available—on line or wherever.

A support group for parents where they can bring their issues and gain insight for parenting.

The four content focuses noted in Chapter 7 also apply to what we need to provide for parents in their home nurturing. This will not be an easy task for the local church for there are many reasons that parents might resist help, but when offered in the proper framework parents will be hungry for the help.

Worship

Worship has a special place in nurture in that it is here that the majority of the congregation gathers each week. It is here that the flow of the Christian life is rehearsed and hopefully picked up by the people. It is here that the major themes and movements of the congregation's life are presented with the hope of involving everyone in them. It is here that the Gospel issues are presented on an ongoing basis and related to everyday life. It would be very effective if what is presented in worship is supported and expanded upon by what happens elsewhere in the church's programming and vice versa.

Congregational worship is a large group setting and is, of course, very different from other settings and takes a different perspective. It is not usual that the folks planning for nurture (in the past "education") have anything to do with worship, but that needs to change. Not that worship would not continue to be planned by church staff and a worship committee, but hopefully these folks would be open to input from other arenas so that there could be more cooperative designing over all the ministries. (See section on the Design Process)

In worship, the task is to help the persons, individually and/or as a community, to get in touch with where they are in their relationship with God in light of the focus of the worship for that time. Hopefully the service order will then move them from there to what God is saying to them about where they are and then what we individually and together are called to do about that in our lives in the coming days.

The Sacraments are tremendously helpful times for nurture but only if our people understand the symbols and the inner meaning of what they are doing. This means that there should be other times, if not within the service, when the sacraments are opened up spiritually and people are helped to see the inner dynamic of the water, the bread and the wine/juice.

Don't forget the planning of small group worship experiences within a retreat or seminar setting. Those are potential nurture experiences also, so the planning should take into account the design of the setting of which it is a part and the intention of the retreat or seminar.

The Sunday School

We cannot do without considering one of the most discussed settings—Sunday School. Over forty years ago there was much discussion whether the Sunday School was still a viable setting for Christian education. There was also a great deal of discussion about alternate settings and where Christian education could most effectively take place. As we know, the Sunday School is still around because we still have that other hour or two on Sunday mornings around the worship time that we can use to gather people together. We do need to continually be open to trying new things and maybe some day we will find the need to move beyond what we now know as Sunday School. Until then we need to see what we can do to improve what we have.

In my denomination the attendance in Sunday School has slowly dropped for various reasons, the main one being, in my opinion, the lack of attention we have paid to the importance of long range nurture efforts and the demise of Christian education as a main ministry of the Church, along with the drop in church attendance in general. We have sought ways to improve that hour and make it more attractive. We have tried campaigns to pump up attendance—which have not worked. Many churches have gone to the "rotation" style of setting for children on Sunday morning, which is simply a large-scale "center" method for teaching. It has yielded some attendance gains in some situations, but seems to have waned in importance in recent years.

Too many of our efforts have been efforts to simply attract people, especially the children and youth. We have sought to entertain rather than truly nurture. We have sought to appeal to what parents and others think we should do rather than paying attention to what is important to do for good, effective Christian nurture.

Let me stop my critical remarks, however, and try to make some suggestions for Sunday School. First, if nothing is happening that is meaningful, of course, the people of whatever age will not come. Remember that our task is not to be successful, but to be faithful—faithful, in this case, to meaningfully and carefully nurture our people in the faith. Being faithful means paying attention to our leadership and their ability, to the content of the experiences both in their relevance as well as being enjoyable and loving. No newfangled method that comes down the pike will substitute for faithful people who are committed to nurture others, who are loving and who have been given the training and the resources to do the best they can do.

One of the great knotty issues in resourcing the Sunday School is the question of what "curriculum resources" should we use. I believe the time has come for each congregation to get serious about developing its own curriculum and the resources to support it. This goes with my contention that the local church must begin to take full responsibility for its nurture. You may, of course, use some purchased resource as a beginning point. I find so many of those resources lacking, however, in one way or another, so it is critical that the local church leaders work through a process of deciding what we want our children and youth to learn and then building a curriculum that we can truly get behind. I suggest using the church year and the comments made above about general nurture experiences to plan what we do in Sunday School. This is serious business and we can no longer limp along just doing what is easiest and ultimately ineffective. If the congregation takes ownership of what happens, I believe we will have fewer problems getting leaders and more energy in providing nurture that is effective.

There may be the issue of disagreement over what the "curriculum" should be so it will take some careful work to involve the key people in the planning and then have some kind of "authority" to say that this is what we will use given the understanding that it will continually be reevaluated over time.

The issue of age grouping is important to carefully consider especially in situations where there are only a few children or youth. To have a broadly graded group takes a little more expertise, but it can still be relevant if done properly. The narrower the age grouping the better but that is not always possible. Having intergenerational classes where adults and children and youth are all together can be an enriching experience, again, if managed in the right way.

I do urge you to find someone who is experienced and skilled in Christian nurture to consult with you on curriculum design for Sunday School, even when you are beginning with a purchased resource as the foundation. There are some things that we need help in knowing how to do. So call your Conference Office and ask for someone who will consult with you. We have looked at some of these issues in the section on designing, but the point is that we simply are called to use what we have to reach and grow our people and do it well.

Small Groups

In the last 25 or so years there has come about the push for small groups, accountability groups, Wesleyan groups, and more. These efforts, in many ways, have been attached to the mechanics of the church growth movement and more as ways to get people involved than to do in-depth nurture. Of course small groups have been around as long as the church has been in existence. In many ways the Sunday School is a small group setting except in certain instances where you have very large classes. For our purposes I am using the term for small groups that take place at times besides the "Sunday School Hour."

Church leaders have referred a great deal to Wesley's use of small cell groups in the Methodist movement, and there is no doubt that small groups are a powerful tool for nurture. The important issue is what you are trying to do with small groups and how you maintain them. Small groups are a method, a way of bringing people together to accomplish what we intend; they are not the end it self. The deep value of small groups is that they can provide an environment in which people can share intimately if they are properly led. The number of people in a small group is such that all can feel involved and be involved because they don't get lost in the size that comes with a large group. Of course, some people like to get lost and they may not take advantage of the small group experience at first and have to be helped to get involved in one.

We can think of small groups having four basic purposes: 1. a setting in which to teach content; 2. a setting for nurturing inner spiritual growth; 3. a setting for creating community; and 4. a setting through which to do intentional service projects. Of course, some groups will function in more than one of these ways at the same time. We could also include administrative groups as small groups for nurture if we so design what happens there, which would be an excellent practice.

Small groups are especially helpful in building community and promoting deeper sharing. An optimum size for a sharing group is not larger than 8 people in my experience and 6 is better. Of course, the smaller the group the more likely that you will have fewer people because not everyone will be there all the time. When the number gets down to 2 or 3 the process has to be reconsidered. The purpose of the group is determinative of how many you can or need to have. I had a spiritual growth group of originally 7 persons in the class, but because of what we were doing in the follow-up group's spiritual direction format, we still had a meaningful sharing if only 2 people came. If you are planning for spiritual direction groups, you should think of having only 3 or 4 in a group. If you are seeking to teach a body of information, a group can get too small for meaningful interaction and the nature of what you are doing has to change. Small "buzz" groups of 2 or 3 and even interaction centers, however, can be used meaningfully within a large class setting to enable more personal interaction as a part of the total experience, but that gets us into the arena of group process. Group leadership ability is of great importance in any group so training and preparation of the leadership is essential.

Often we think of small groups in terms of some of the small group programs that have come along in recent years—covenant discipleship, groups, etc. They all can be helpful or not depending upon how they are managed and depending, of course, on your intention for nurture. Many people have tried the "neighborhood" group structure just to get people together for building community and shepherding each other. The process of structuring the groups is very important as is the way of maintaining the groups over time. (The details of such management is beyond the scope of this writing.) Such a structure can be used helpfully on a short term basis—gathering folks for 6 sessions or so over a couple months (or more) for instance in order build a common understanding and sharing around a major issue confronting the congregation or as a major nurture effort in a season of the church year.

Again, as with any method, the use of small groups is just that, a method, but as such they are an essential part of our Christian experience and should be used effectively any chance we get.

Service/Mission Experiences

Remember that settings for nurture also include the service experiences when they include some form of reflection/training time. Too often we go on such trips or local experiences and never gather the group to discuss our reasons for doing it, something about the people we touch and the ways in which God has touched us or not.

The preparation for a service experience must include time for understanding the people we are serving and the nature of our task as servants. The time should include prayer in which we are able to listen for what it is that God is calling us to do in this situation and then sharing around what comes from that time. Another helpful pre-service experience would be some form of commitment or commission ritual at a worship time. When done well such experiences provide a way for the individual to confirm their inner intention or will toward a particular project.

During the experience it will be crucial to spend time "debriefing" the day's experience spiritually as well as how well we did and the technical problems to be dealt with. Then after returning, another time spent with some silence as well as sharing to become open to how the individuals feel about the experience, what they learned about being servants and how they experienced the Spirit in it all.

Large Groups

Large assemblies, of course, are best for communicating information to large numbers at a time. They become important when we have a resource person who will only be with us for a brief time and we want as many as possible to take advantage of their presence. The effectiveness of the nurture that is possible is increased in large groups when we use some form of "break out" groups or buzz groups to process what people are hearing. The ability to do that will depend upon the presenter's style and what he/she is willing to work out with you. I hope that you will do everything you can to make such experiences as effective as possible by the use of such group process methods.

One of the real challenges we have had, in the past at least, is the very large Sunday school class that is taught by a charismatic leader who simply lectures. There is some modicum of nurture going on, but its long-range effectiveness is questionable. That is especially true when the content of what is taught is irrelevant to the needs of the group and the message of the Gospel. There is not much we can do with such groups that have been going on for a long time, but we can make an effort to set up a different framework and method for any such group that starts in the future. In some cases it may be possible to influence the content of what is "taught" in the groups.

Chapter 11

Methodology

Methodology is directly related to what I have called the key experiences because those experiences are carried out though methods. There are more or less effective methods for information communication. There are more or less helpful methods to use in a sharing session, etc. Methods are important because in themselves, they implement the experience by involving the participant more fully in what is happening. A method can contribute positively or negatively to the relational environment of the experience. A method can make the difference between whether someone really interacts with the content of the experience or is just a "bystander."

My perception is that we have ceased to see methods from an overall perspective as tools that form a crucial aspect of the implementation of our task. Too often we only find methods as they are attached to a certain kind of program and do not understand methods as a set of tools that can be learned and used in many different settings. We have come to see methods as programs. The use of small groups, for instance, is a method, but we have turned it into a program. In addition and because of how we see them, we don't seem to train folks in methods much any more—there again, that is my perception. I hope that I am wrong.

I was brought up in ministry in a time when we truly focused on training in the latest methods. These were not tied to some new fad technique, but were basic teaching/learning practices. It was a time when there was sociological research and training going on in education around the training of leaders in things like interpersonal communication skills, group management methods, etc. There were certain methods such as using centers in young children's groups that were taught as the way we need to do it because centers were found to be the most effective for the age level, which is still the case.

There is so much that sociological research has provided that seeks to bring greater effectiveness to our nurture settings. Those methods and skills are available and I propose that if we don't already use them, then we need to go back to them. Some of them, I am sure, you use without thinking about it. What are you missing?

What do I refer to as methods? I think of group process methods such as buzz groups where you ask people to talk with one or two others for a few minutes to process a presented idea, circle response where you go around the circle for responses so as to not leave individuals out unless they want to pass, how to lead a discussion and keep everyone involved. I think of using panels, listening teams, research and report, work groups, learning centers, role-playing, simulation games, laboratory training, art, computer-aided instruction. There are detailed methods for getting acquainted and for evaluation. How and when you use any of these methods is determined by the age group and what you are seeking to accomplish.

As I said, you may have learned to use some of these, and I hope that you also think about which is the most effective method as you are planning and experimenting with some that you don't use that much.

Methods and the People

Methods, by their nature, are more helpful to certain people than others. This is especially true—and you know this implicitly—when we talk about age levels. The methods for a young children's class will be very different from those for an adult class though there are some exceptions. For instance, it is very important to use centers for young children. Centers can also be an effective method for an adult group, but you would not use lecture for young children.

Methods also extend to how we guide the individuals in an experience in relationship to their needs and level of experience or understanding. A group of persons that are new to each other will need more opportunity for group building. A group that is less mature in the faith will need a certain kind of approach in which there is openness to questions without anyone feeling unaccepted. A group working on deeply personal spiritual issues will need careful leading in how to share without trying to fix each other.

There is also a range of personal skills that are very helpful in working with groups and individuals. Some of the most important kinds of skills I learned were those involved in what was called "interpersonal competency," skills in how relate to one another. They included skills such as active listening, giving feedback, reading nonverbal communication and perception checking. These skills are still important for us today and especially as we seek to help persons to know how important they are.

Planning A Session for Learning

Let's take a little diversion into a specific aspect of methodology. One of the short forms of how to design a teaching/learning session that I learned in those days when we talked more about methods has stayed with me over the years, and it is helpful because it points up the importance of methods and how to use them. The design process goes like this:

Determine your goal or objective for the session.

Decide on the input and the method for delivering the input

Plan for a time in interaction with the input.

Plan the time of sharing.

Be sure to talk about "so what" and evaluate the session.

Notice the five elements in a session: goal, input, interaction, sharing, evaluation. Each one of these takes some thought as to the methods we want to use as well as the order in which they come. Some brief comments about each of them:

Goal: What is it that you want the persons to be able to do, understand, etc., after the session is over? You need to identify exactly what the topic is for the session and limit the goals to only one or two if this is an hour-long session. The following actions then would be designed to fulfill that goal.

Input: Does the input come from outside or from within the group? Will it be used ahead of the group time or within the session? What form will it take: printed, audio/visual, lecture, individual presentation, etc. Please remember that an audio/visual is not the whole session, it is a method. Only in very special circumstances should we use a DVD or video that takes up all the time and leaves none for interaction and sharing. I think video presentations should take up no more than 1/4 to 1/3 of the session time, leaving enough for interaction. Lecture is the least effective method but may be the best way under certain circumstances, but again interaction is critical.

Interaction may be the one aspect of a learning session that is least dealt with creatively. People only absorb something that they interact with. It is important that we cause folks to think critically about what they are receiving and get inside of it with their minds. Asking folks key questions to share with each other about, a writing assignment, role-playing, art—there are lots of ways to provide for interaction so do more than simply open the group for questions, although that is also important.

Sharing is a way of allowing persons to become aware of what they are thinking by talking about how they have interacted with the input. It can be done in a number of ways but always to increase the ability of each person to have a chance to share.

Evaluation or "so what": This is a time to simply look at what has happened in the session and see what it has meant to the group. It may also be a time to talk about what we want to do with what we have heard/learned/shared relating to action beyond the group time.

Using Information Technology

Finally a word about one of the big methodologies of today's world, that of information technology: the internet, DVD's, CD's, email, etc. When videotaped content hit the stage to take over 16 mm movie film and slide projectors, every one thought we had the answer. It was not THE answer, but only an answer as are all of the other media resources at our disposal. The big difference is that now more and more people have access to the internet and email so that it creates a medium for information exchange we have never seen before. We are already using these resources by having church web sites, sending out group emails, etc. There are folks encouraging us to use what we find on the internet for curriculum resources for our nurture experiences.

We must remember that these are potential resources, not the final answer to what we need. We must use them where they are effective and not try to make them do everything. We also have to be selective of those resources since some will not fit what we seek to do or are of poor quality and unhelpful or even have harmful content. Not everything on the internet is something we should use.

Many experts have also noted the problem of using media where there is no face-to-face contact without some way of getting people together. Personal relationship and contact is essential for Christian community, but there is a place for using such media to reach out to people that otherwise we would never touch and whom we can then invite to be a part of a group.

There is great potential for leadership development through the use of online courses and DVDs to train leaders for Christian nurture. It is hoped that more such resources will become available in the near future.

CHAPTER 12

LEADERSHIP DEVELOPMENT

Of all things to be said about leadership of nurture ministry, or any ministry for that matter, is that the leader's spiritual maturity is fundamental. I am not talking here about some mechanical evaluation of people's spirituality, but simply about whether they are involved in their own journey of nurturing their personal relationship with God. I don't think that we can go around being dogmatic about this, but we can be sensitive when we are inviting leaders that are on that journey in some way or not. Of course, this also implies that we who invite the leaders are involved in our own journeys into God's love.

A word about staff leadership

First of all, it is doubtful we will ever return to local churches having full-time paid persons in this specialized ministry. So what is said here will apply to a very few, but the theory still holds and could be applied to any paid staff person.

It has become a vision of mine that staff leadership for nurture needs to move out of the realm of simply guiding an "educational" program and instead become a "consultant" in nurture for all of the ministries of the church, even worship. This assumes that that person has been trained in the theology and practice of nurture to be able to provide help and guidance for the various ministries so that what happens there is effective in its nurture aspects as well as its main task. I realize that such a concept will have difficulty due to "turf" issues, but maybe some day it will be possible. Seeing nurture potential in all of our ministries is, however, also a very strong reason for doing a better job in training our pastors in effective nurture practice.

As to the volunteer leadership for nurture there are certainly no magic wands we can use on leadership development. It simply calls for some good, hard thinking and planning and then hard work. All of these suggestions will, of course, have to be adjusted in light of the size of the congregation and resources available.

First, it is critical to lay a foundational environment where nurture is seen as a central task of the congregation. All congregations have something that seems to be their key ministry, some area in which they have definite strengths and that is as it should be. If nurture is not a strong suit in a congregation, for it to come to see it as a central ministry will take some extra time and effort, and there is no one thing that will necessarily accomplish it. It may be to simply make a point to lift up what is happening in the Sunday School and in other settings. It may be important to make a special effort to get new members involved in some kind of nurture setting as quickly as possible to give the message that this is something you hold as very important. There is always the special day in the fall called Christian Education Sunday that is still observed in UMC congregations where those who lead in nurture efforts are recognized. Certainly the pastor's attention is critical where he/she takes the time to mention the nurture opportunities as being of great importance. Most fundamentally, does your congregation set high expectations for the quality of the ministry of nurture? Is there real time and effort spent in designing and resourcing the ministry along with high expectations in the training of leaders? Spend some time thinking about what it would take in your congregation for nurture to take its rightful place.

It makes a difference to have a strong adult nurturing program that gives people the understanding and sense of commitment to ministry that will make it possible for them to become a leader in nurture ministries. If we want people who can nurture others in our congregations, we have to raise them up through their own experience in being nurtured in the faith. This may be simply an emphasis on adult nurture opportunities in general, or it may go further and be a special set of opportunities to which we invite potential leaders.

The best leaders are ones who are discovered and carefully invited, not who are received through an open invitation to just anyone to serve. It seems easier to just ask for anyone that's interested, but it can also be a way of getting persons into leadership who should not be there, who are just using the opportunity to build up their own ego; they will cause more difficulty than help. There should be a process of looking through the congregation for those who are involved in growing themselves, and those that are known for their spiritual maturity. They should be invited by personal invitation, through a phone call or a personal letter to start with. Invite them to investigate the possibility, giving them the terms of service and what will be expected of them and what they can expect in the way of support.

All this means that the congregation will have to set some quality standards—expectations of the leader and of those who manage the ministry. Here are some things that I think are basic expectations:

First, I deeply believe that we have to stop recruiting leaders for part-time, rotating leadership in children and youth nurture where there is a different person each Sunday in a month, for instance, or every other Sunday, etc. If our nurture for children and youth is to be truly effective, we must have persons who will commit to being there every Sunday for a year and then have substitutes who can serve when they need to be gone. The children and youth need that kind of stability in their leadership. At the end of each year the leader can be re-invited for another year or can take time off. This provides a release valve for unhelpful situations as well as an assurance that no one will be "stuck" with the job forever.

Second, recruit teams of 2 or 3 people for each group wherever possible. I know this is more difficult, but it will increase the willingness of people to serve and increase our effectiveness. It is also a safety issue when something happens in the class that should make having more than one person a basic requirement.

Third, always, always have a list of substitutes that the regular leaders can call when they need to be absent.

Fourth, be sure to have someone who will be present on Sunday mornings or other times to provide support and help in procuring resources during the week as well as on Sundays. We used to have "superintendents" and "counseling teachers" who served this function until we forgot that was important.

Fifth, allow leaders to have access to their rooms to set up, etc., when the church office might not be open, since so many of our leaders will work during the week.

Sixth, but far from last, there is training. The leaders should be expected to be involved in a certain period of training that is the most convenient for all concerned and that is a requirement for being a leader. This is a real sticking point for many because it is so difficult to get people to attend training. We will never increase the effectiveness of what we do until we expect this of our leaders and stick with it. I believe that in the long haul it will increase the ability to find leaders as well as the quality of our nurture because it sends a message that this is important, that it has status in the church, and it helps overcome the sense of inadequacy of those we recruit. Such training should cover the objective of nurture, what it is that we are trying to accomplish as well as training in the skills of leading a group and using the appropriate resources. They must know that we are not just asking them to "do" the curriculum resources we hand them, but to actually be responsible for the nurture of those in their group. How the training takes place certainly should make use of the technology of today. Can it be done with DVD resources, with teleconferences with people in their homes, through online courses? We have to use our ingenuity and hard work to make it happen. The local church may also have to go outside itself to find the help in doing the training and locating the resources for training. The help is there if you ask for it. I know that churches need it and it can be found, but you have to contact your conference office and locate the help. Some of that help might take a little money, but it might not, so ask!

It seems that to involve the leaders of the groups in planning what happens will increase effectiveness and build a sense of importance of the task and their abilities as leaders. People who are included in planning are more responsible for what happens. For instance, have a planning session each three months where all of the leaders for a particular age group would come together to talk and plan what will happen in the months ahead, to coordinate efforts with the larger church or between groups, to locate resources and to deal with problems.

Finally, but of great importance, leaders need some kind of congregational recognition that is meaningful and that raises the status of their work and of the ministry as a whole in the eyes of the congregation. This can be done as a part of worship and also in a special recognition service. Maybe there is a plaque on the wall in the main gathering area where the names of people who have served in nurture are presented along with their years of service.

Many of these ideas apply more directly to leaders who nurture children and youth, and that is where we usually need the most people. Leaders of adult groups bring a different set of issues, though the above ideas can be very relevant in a short-term program of adult nurture. Many adult classes that are on-going social groups usually come up with their own leaders, but from time to time they come looking for someone new or in addition to the ones they have. Whatever the size of your church it will be important to begin to develop people who can lead adult groups. Maybe there are persons in your congregation who have some specific areas of expertise who would be able to share how their faith interacts with that area of life. Maybe they have some special courses they have taught that they could offer. The important thing to do would be to provide a way to help these potential leaders to gain some understanding of the Gospel and the scriptures through which they could filter what they know and make some very relevant contribution to the nurture of adults. Maybe you could develop an "adult nurture faculty" of persons (from one to several persons) who are capable to lead certain courses. Some of the new DVD-based courses can more easily be led by persons with only a basic understanding of leading group sharing, as long as they have a good grounding in the faith.

Let me say a word about a vision that I have expressed at various times. That vision is to begin to see our nurture leaders as "spiritual guides" not as "teachers." To do so puts a whole different frame around how we see the person's task and how we choose the leader and how we train him or her. Such a vision puts the emphasis where it needs to be, on the leader guiding people in their spiritual journeys. Such a vision also would make a tremendous difference in how leaders see their task and would, I think, give them a much greater sense of ministry in what they are doing. I have included in the Appendix an article that I wrote some time ago describing this vision in more detail.

I realize that some of you who have been around a long time will recognize these ideas as old ones, but I don't know what would be better. If you do know better ones then please use them. I have been "around the horn" many times with these ideas trying to use them with varying degrees of success and failure and realize the problems and difficulties involved. I also realize that this takes people to pull it off, which means either the pastor in very small situations, committed laity in others, or staff in larger situations. All of these ideas have to be shaped to fit where you are. As I said about training, you may need to ask for help and you should not be afraid to do so. Whatever the barriers, I still believe that if we commit ourselves to quality and effectiveness as a measure of our faithfulness to God's call, then we can make these things or something better work where we are.

END NOTES

1. Westerhoff, John W. III, New York: Seabury Press, 1976.
2. Westerhoff, John W., III, *Living the Faith Community*, New York: Seabury, 2004.
3. If you would like a very helpful picture of the "demise," you can find one in Charles Foster's new book *From Generation to Generation*.
4. This evaluation is from an informal survey I conducted of the annual conference websites in three jurisdictions of the United Methodist Church.
5. Thomas R. Kelly, *A Testament of Devotion*, New York: Harper and Row, 1941.
6. St. Teresa of Avila, *The Interior Castle*, Translation by Mirabai Starr, Riverhead Books, 2003, p. 44.
7. Norma Thompson, "Religious Education: Theory and Practice," *Religious Education*, Vol. 79, No. 1, Winter 1984, p. 51.
8. Richard Rohr, *The Naked Now*, Crossroads, 2009, p. 82.
9. If you are interested in the view of these issues of the human problem held by John Wesley, you might want to look at the lecture by Albert Outler now found in *Evangelism and Theology in the Wesleyan Spirit*, pp. 89-101. I think you will find that the above fits well with Wesley.
10. This is not a simple issue, however, in that mental illness also can play a part in our behavior problems.

11. Palmer, Parker, *A Hidden Wholeness*, Jossy-Bass, San Francisco, 2004.

12. Groome, Thomas, *Sharing Faith*, Harper Collins, New York, NY 1991.

13. It is interesting to compare the three movements I have proposed with Outler's statement of Wesley's prescription for spiritual growth: "(1) repentance (self-knowledge), (2) renunciation of self-will, and (3) faith (trust in God's sheer, unmerited grace)." See *Evangelism and Theology in the Wesleyan Spirit*, p. 98.

14. John Wesley, Sermon 10, "The Witness of the Spirit 1," p. 18.

15. Evelyn Underhill, *The Essentials of Mysticism*, One World Publications, 1995, pp. 150-151.

16. Fowler, James, *Stages of Faith*, Harper and Row, 1981.

17. Teresa of Avila, *The Interior Castle*, Mirabai Starr, Trans., Riverhead Books, 2003.

18. Rohr, Richard, *The Naked Now*, Crossroads, 2009.

19. Erikson, Erik, *Childhood and Society*, W.W. Norton and Company, 1993.

20. Meyers, Robin, *The Underground Church*, Jossey-Bass, San Francisco, 2012, p. 130 ff.

RESOURCES

There are so many resources out there and I encourage you to look for them. Here are a few that I think are most appropriate to mention in following up what is above:

For a source of help for a variety of issues
> Be sure to go to the web site of United Methodist Church Discipleship Ministries at **www.umcdiscipleship.org**
> There you will find many suggested materials, resources, ideas for leader development, and can sign up for a regular email resource from staff members.

For a guide to a planning/designing process:
> *Charting a Course of Discipleship*
> Teresa Gilbert, Patty Johansen, and Jay Regennitter.
> Discipleship Resources, 2012.
> Available at **UpperRoom.org/bookstore**
> The web site at **www.faithformation2020.net** has information for a view of making use of what is on the Internet, but remember that you have to decide what is helpful or not.

For another look at doing nurture in the whole congregation:
> *From Generation To Generation: The Adaptive Challenge Of Mainline Protestant Education In Forming Faith*

Foster, Charles R.
Cascade Books, 2012.

You might want to check out two older books by John H. Westerhoff:
Will Our Children Have Faith?
Westerhoff, John H.
Seabury Press, 1976.
Living The Faith Community: The Church That Makes A Difference
Westerhoff, John H.
Winston Press, 1985.

Recent books about Christian nurture:
Discovering Discipleship: Dynamics Of Christian Education
Blevins, Dean Gray, and Mark A. Maddix.
Beacon Hill Press of Kansas City, 2010.
Will There Be Faith?: A new vision for educating and growing disciples
Groome, Thomas H.
HarperOne, 2011.
Teaching the Way of Jesus
Seymour, Jack L. Abingdon, 2014.

Books that are helpful as a background for nurture in the future:
The Future of Faith
Cox, Harvey. HarperOne, 2009.
Almost Christian: What the Faith of Our Teenagers is Telling the American Church
Creasy Dean, Kenda.
Oxford University Press, 2010.
Christianity After Religion: The End Of Church And The Birth Of A New Spiritual Awakening
Bass, Diana Butler.
HarperOne, 2012.
The Great Emergence: How Christianity Is Changing And Why
Tickle, Phyllis.
Baker Books, 2008.

Learning Together in the Christian Fellowship
Little, Sara.
John Knox Press, 1956.
A little book that was a classic about group dynamics and teaching methods—if you can find a copy.

Appendix A

Themes for Seasons

Here are some ideas for themes to use in designing nurture in the seasons of the Church Year. Each one of these themes contains many sub-themes that could be developed over the years. You will also think of others—this is certainly not an exhaustive list.

Advent and Christmastide
   Our Expectations and Hopes for Our Lives
   The Incarnation
   The Nature of God's Love

Epiphany
   Baptism
   Church Membership
   The Mission of the Church
   Faith and Science
   Who is Jesus for Us?

Lent
   Self-Understanding
   The Human Problem
   Prayer and Our Relationship with God
   What We Need in Life

Facing Death in order to Live Fully

Eastertide (Easter thru May)
Resurrection and New Life
The Fruits of the Spirit—Life Lived in the Spirit
The Family
Parenting
The Sacrament of the Lord's Supper

Pentecost (June-August)
The Nature of the Church
Church History
Relationships
The Holy Spirit

Kingdomtide (Sept.-Advent, or we can continue Pentecost)
The Law and Faith
The Commandments and The Teachings of Jesus
The Nature of the Kingdom of God
What is God's Will
Issues of Justice and Peace

APPENDIX B

THE TEACHER AS SPIRITUAL GUIDE

by R. Ben Marshall

(The following article was printed in the magazine, "Leader in the Church School Today," for December-January-February 2001 and 2002, Cokesbury, with some slight editorial differences.)

We are entering a new era in the arena of Christian Nurture. This new era is a result of the deep spiritual hunger that is making itself known in our country and the recent emphasis on "spiritual formation" … prayer, spiritual life retreats, spiritual direction, etc. We have even begun to change the term "Christian Education" to "Christian Formation." Therefore we need to begin to think seriously about what this means for the role of those who have been leaders ("teachers," "youth counselors," etc.) in the ministry of Christian education in our churches.

Let's look quickly at what the title "teacher" implies. First of all it comes to us from a long history of seeing the role of the Sunday School as one of "teaching," of imparting information that will then engender faith. It may also be that behind the role of teaching is the concept that "faith" is "believing in" a theological affirmation about God and Jesus Christ. The teaching then is toward understanding the affirmations and coming to believe in them. Certainly this is a crucial role that must take place in the nurturing of faith. But it is not the only role nor the central one.

We must begin to see our task as more one of helping persons to enter into a personal relationship with God who loves them. People must be helped to engender a trust in God's unconditional love for them and to learn how to go about continuing to nurture that loving relationship throughout their lives. At the same time, that person must come to know, at every age, what it means to be loving in his/her world.

Certainly the imparting of information and engendering of understanding is crucial here, but the focus is not on the information but on the person's trust in God's love. Faith in this view is "trusting in God's love" as the center piece of intellectual belief and active love, for it is God's love that will change us into loving persons.

I am proposing, then, that we begin to see ourselves as "spiritual guides" rather than teachers. The Christian Life is a spiritual journey with God, into God's love. A Guide is someone who is also on the Journey and will invite the others to join in that Journey, helping them along the way in whatever way they particularly need to be helped.

People of all ages do have a spiritual hunger, a hunger for the God who Loves them and wants them to find that Love. That is no less the case for the young child as it is for the adult who has lost his/her way in life. So the guidance has directly to do with a person's mutually loving relationship with God. A "spiritual" guide is one who is in a relationship with God and who is going about helping others in their own relationships with God. It does not imply some special knowledge, although the more knowledge we have the better we will be able to help, especially in terms of the "helping skills." But it does imply some experience with God or at least a recognition of that relationship and a desire to Journey in it. The relationship with God is THE central issue in our task in these days, both for the one who guides and the one who is being guided.

People are hungry for a relationship with God, but people need someone to help them to become open to that God of Love that Jesus gave his life to call us toward. We really cannot do it alone. If there is anything that the Incarnation means, it is that we need some one who will become a vehicle through which we can become open to God when we cannot do it on our own. We need a Guide.

A Guide, for me, is one who comes to understand me, who comes to know what I need and is willing to spend some time helping me along the Journey. A Guide helps me to know that I am on a Journey, what that Journey is about and what I am really trying to find on this Journey. He or she introduces me to a God who Loves unconditionally and who is always with me seeking to Love me and help me to be able to nurture my relationship with that Loving God on my own as well as with others. A Guide is also someone who helps me to be able to manage the ins and outs of life's difficulties and be able to love under all sorts of circumstances.

So what does all this mean for you, the Teacher, in becoming a Spiritual Guide? (Please remember that anything mentioned below assumes that the development level of the person is taken into account. Not all of the suggestions would apply to every age in all cases.)

First, it means that you become more and more aware of your own personal relationship with God and nurture it. You do have a relationship already. God is seeing to that and is continually inviting you to allow God to love you. You may already be doing what you can do to nurture that relationship or maybe you can do some more. Besides your worship with others, central is your own personal time of prayer. There is no one way to pray, but there is your way to pray. You may want to learn some more about prayer for yourself, but if nothing else, simply begin by spending some regular time with God, by yourself. And along with any scripture or reading you like, spend some of that time just listening with your heart for the Love that God has for you. As you grow in your own relationship, you will be able to help the child or youth or adult in your group with theirs. And helping them just might mean inviting them to begin that personal prayer along with you.

Second, it means that you will seek to be very aware of where the person in your group is needing to be Loved. What would help them to know how important God deems them to be. It might be providing a group or individual activity that is really appropriate for the group's age range. It might be meeting them at the door with a warm and caring welcome, checking on how they are doing?

Third, it means that your group activities include prayer and learning about prayer in ways that are helpful to the particular group with which you work. It might mean giving them a chance to talk about their present insight about their own prayer. We need to help people know how to pray so that they feel free to use whatever form is best for them, assured that God lovingly receives all our prayers. And certainly helping them to learn to listen for God's loving them. Maybe they need to experience some silent listening as a group or even a time to pray individually within the group time. Remember that it is God who does the nurturing within the person; we only provide the situation in which the person can become more open to that Nurturing Love from God.

Fourth, it means that God and our relationship with God becomes a central focus of the content of the group time. Not in a heavy or authoritarian way, because that does not communicate God's Love. But in a natural way, so that the persons come to realize that God is real and functions in every part of their lives. You may want to spend some time now and then, when appropriate, letting the individuals talk about their own personal relationship with God and what it means to them.

Fifth, it certainly means there will be times when you share some information and understanding through the Scriptures that help them to learn the stories of how God loves us, and what it means to be loving through hearing about how Jesus loved and what he taught about loving. In other words, do a little content "teaching" using the best methods possible. Let me remind you, however, that in our use of Scriptures, we must remember that certain passages may actually communicate an idea about God that we do not intend, either because it is a very difficult passage to understand or the age level of the persons makes them unable to understand the ideas intended. So we need to choose carefully if we are to truly help our group encounter the God of Unconditional Love.

Finally, but not least by any means, as guides we will help them into experiences of loving behavior. It may simply be how we help them to relate to others in their group. It will certainly be done by the way we treat them. It will hopefully include some way to involve them in service to others beyond their group.

You will rightly note that a lot of what I have said is about things that you are probably doing already—I hope that is the case. But I hope that you have caught the shift in focus from a concern about information or idea content to the relationship with God, a shift that moves us from being only teachers to being spiritual guides. What we do in the Sunday School must focus on the Spirit, God the Holy Spirit, and let that focus give direction and shape to the teaching and the training and the service that we do.

What we are about is helping persons to be able to enter into and nurture a relationship with God that will sustain them throughout their lives, through the temptations and challenges they surely will encounter. Such help must depend upon God's work with us and with them or else we are missing our task. And for this they need a Guide!

About the Author

R. Ben Marshall is a retired United Methodist Elder and Minister of Christian Education. Ben has a Doctor of Ministry in Christian Education from Perkins School of Theology and a certificate in spiritual direction from Shalem Institute for Spiritual Formation. He has served in various capacities in Christian education for over 50 years with experience in all age levels in medium and large congregations and at the annual conference level. He is a member of the United Methodist Association of Scholars in Christian Education, the Religious Education Association and Christians Engaged in Faith Formation. He has been a trainer in Christian education at the Conference and General church level and has been providing spiritual direction for over 20 years. Ben is presently residing in Dallas, Texas, with his wife Karan and is teaching adults at Northaven UMC in Dallas.

Printed in the United States
By Bookmasters